Scrum Fundamentals

for

ScrumAlliance ® Certified ScrumMaster ®

Certification

The *Pass Certification Assessments at the First Attempt* Series

Each book in this series provides a *single, comprehensive* source of information on how to pass select *Certification Assessments*. This information includes relevant details on the Certification/Assessment, a strategy to prepare for and take the assessment, and finally, adequate study material for the assessment itself.

By September 2015, this guidance will available for *Scrum Master* Certification as well as *PMI® Project Management Professional (PMP)®* Certification. Guidance for other certifications, such as *Scrum Product Owner, PMI® Certified Associate in Project Management (CAPM)®*, and *PMI® Professional in Business Analysis Certification (PBA)®* will be available later in the year.

Initially, this guidance is available only in the form of books (printed/eBook). By December 2015, interactive *Instructor-led* and *self-paced **eLearning courses*** will be introduced on various platforms.

Of the currently available books in this series, the first three are targeted at those who *have a basic/intermediate knowledge of Scrum*, while the last one is for those who *may not have any knowledge of Scrum*.

Vol 1: Scrum Fundamentals for ScrumAlliance ® Certified ScrumMaster ® Certification: *Pass the CSM Assessment in One Week*

Vol 2: Scrum Fundamentals for Scrum.org Professional Scrum Master I Certification*: Pass the PSM I Assessment in One Week*

Vol 3: Scrum Fundamentals for Scrum Master Certification*: Pass the CSM/PSM I Assessments in One Week*

Vol 4: Scrum Fundamentals for Beginners*: Pass the CSM/PSM I Assessments in One Month*

For more information, please send an email to: **xyepress@xyberg.com**

Scrum Fundamentals

for

ScrumAlliance ® ScrumMaster ®

Certification

Feroz Khan

CSM, PSM I, PMP

Table of Contents

List of Tables and Figures

About the Author

Feroz's passion for software development started in 1984, while still in high school, when he was first exposed to a *Sinclair ZX Spectrum* home computer by a friend. Since there were only a few universities offering a graduate program in Computers in 1985, he joined the graduate program in *Electronics and Telecommunication Engineering* at *Panjab University*. Aside from attending several formal courses in Computers and Software Programming, which were part of the graduate program, he spent bulk of his time developing computer programs. Since then, he has witnessed (and participated in) four stages of development of the IT industry: *Standalone PCs & basic networks*, *Client/Server applications*, *Internet*, and *Mobility*.

Over a career spanning approximately 20 years, he has worked as a Developer, IT/Systems Analyst, Project Manager, Program Manager, Delivery Manager and Engagement/Account Manager for few leading global Software Services companies. He has led several hundreds of projects, large and small, developing enterprise solutions for startups, SMEs and Fortune 500 companies. Most of these were BI/data warehousing, eCommerce, SaaS, EAI/BPI, or enterprise solutions integrated to ERP systems, developed using a wide range of tools, technologies and platforms.

His formal experience in the industry started in early 1996, with a stint at *International Data Corporation (India)*, after completing his MBA. As an *IT Market Analyst*, he conducted several market research studies; authored Reports on emerging segments of the Indian IT industry; and edited the SAARC section of the *South Asia Report* published by *IDC, Hong Kong*.

From early 1998 until late 2002, as Systems Analyst and Project Manager at *Globsyn Technologies*, he led a large development team to deliver a wide variety of projects, using ISO-certified *Agile* and *Waterfall* methodologies, including the *Rational Unified Process*. Most of the clients were US-based small/midsized companies or startups. He and his team helped to convert their concepts to market ready products in the areas of eCommerce and EAI/BPI for the Telecom industry.

In the next phase of his career, from late 2002 through 2015, he worked with a few leading IT Services companies, such as *Zensar Technologies*, *Saama Technologies* and *Tech Mahindra* in various Engagement, Delivery and Account Management roles for several Fortune 100 customers. He has actively led a delivery team of 200-300 associates, while with *Zensar* and *Tech Mahindra*, for a number of projects at *Cisco Systems* and *Apple Computers*, respectively.

While with *Zensar*, his team has developed and supported hundreds of custom applications for the *Corporate Compliance*, *Corporate Quality*, *Engineering Quality*, *Manufacturing*, *Supply Chain*, *Software Enablement* organizations of *Cisco*. During this period, he championed, and mentored several teams on, the implementation of *Use Case* and *Six Sigma* methodologies. In 2006, in close association with *Cisco* Managers, he co-developed a *Managed Services* model of delivery for *Zensar*, in which *Cisco* FTEs' involvement was limited to project or strategic oversight. This freed up *Cisco* FTEs to focus on 'core' responsibilities, while bringing costs down considerably without any deterioration in quality. He made a significant contribution in developing the IT Operations processes and model for the *Customer Value Chain* organization led by Cisco Managers and Program Managers. This model was adopted as the *de facto* standard for Global IT Operations. He also led or managed several programs at *Advanced/Consulting Services* and *WebEx* organizations of *Cisco*.

At *WebEx*, as *PMO Program Manager* and *Governance Lead*, he managed a large program, with multiple large releases while being responsible for defining, setting up and governing PPM processes, encompassing Portfolio Management, Program Management and Project Management.

While with *Tech Mahindra*, he worked closely with Directors and Managers in the *Customer Systems*, *GBI* and *Worldwide Retail Commerce* organizations at *Apple*, including the *PoS* group, to improve the quality of the delivery and quality of resources. These entailed definition and adoption of suitable processes and tools for requirements management, agile delivery, unit testing, code reviews and coverage, continuous integration, and test-driven development. Multiple teams in his portfolio were able to successfully adopt Scrum and improve delivery continuously.

During his stint at *Saama*, he managed several *Business Intelligence* and *Analytics* projects for various clients, such as *Cisco, Apple, Wells Fargo, McAfee*, and *JDSU* to name a few.

For a short period in 2004, he joined the *Legislative Data Center (LDC)* at *Sacramento*, as a Consultant to lead the *Business Modeling* and *Requirement Management* disciplines. LDC, the IT department of the *California State Legislature*, was implementing the *Rational Unified Process* for their new *ESI Program*. The program adopted a unique matrix organization based on RUP disciplines. It aimed to completely rewrite over 100 legacy systems, based on almost as many technologies, into a single SOA-based *Enterprise System and Services* solution for the California Legislature, using J2EE primarily.

A few months later, he joined *Informatica* as a *Business Process Analyst* (consultant) to develop business processes for a *Customer Usage Profile* system, which would help to understand how customers use their product and then identify upsell and cross-sell opportunities.

In 2010, Feroz Khan founded *Xyberg Systems*, a stealth startup, which is in the process of developing a product aimed at disrupting the way Enterprises recruit and hire employees; while at the same time, allowing skilled individuals to monetize their talent through their social network. From time to time, he provides IT Consulting Services to Fortune 500 companies, particularly in the areas of methodologies, process design, and program or project execution.

Preface

The idea for this *book series* came about after I realized I had spent an 'incredibly' large amount of time and effort to gather information and gain knowledge on how to attain a *Scrum Master* credential. Most of the time was spent surfing the Internet, browsing for different kinds of information, such as:

- Type of Certifications/Assessments, Costs/Benefits, Requirements, etc.
- Available Training Courses, Course Outlines, Costs/Benefits, Relevance, etc.
- Scope and Source of Knowledge required for these Assessments
- Sample Questions & Answers, Mock Tests, etc.

There is little doubt that the Internet is the best source of information today. However, it has become extremely difficult to weed out the *inaccurate* or *irrelevant* information from the truly valuable one. After several weeks, I realized that only about 25% of my efforts had been productive. It is very easy to get trapped into an almost endless cycle of *searching for* and *reading the content* from various sources of information, such as websites, articles, e-books, and physical books, to name a few. For most of us, who have very little time to spare on a daily basis on any effort outside of work, this could be very frustrating. I am quite sure that you may have undergone a similar experience, if you had decided to embark on a similar exercise.

Imagine, now, that you have a friend who is willing to do all the legwork for you. He or she would spend countless hours 'crawling' through the endless ocean of information; sifting through the good, bad and ugly; and finally, putting together a limited set of distilled information for your rapid consumption. Unfortunately, I did not have such a friend; but this *book series* is an outcome of such a wish.

I am fairly certain that this *book series* may neither address all of the questions you may have, nor provide all of the information you may need; but I am very confident that it will serve the stated objective – help you pass the *Certified ScrumMaster* assessment within one week.

-- Feroz Khan

Part 1: Introduction

This Part provides an overview of **Scrum Assessments & Credentials**, the **Purpose and Audience of the Book Series**, and its **Organization**. This Part is common to all four Scrum Fundamentals books in this Series.

Along with *Jeff McKenna* and *John Scumniotales*, *Jeff Sutherland* created the *Scrum* methodology and started the very first Scrum team at *Easel Corporation* in 1993. *Ken Schwaber*, another founding father of Scrum, formalized the Scrum framework in association with *Jeff Sutherland* and co-authored **The Scrum Guide**. *Ken* was responsible for founding the **Scrum Alliance** and creating the Certified Scrum Master programs and its derivatives. He left the *Scrum Alliance* in the fall of 2009 and then founded **Scrum.org** to 'improve the quality and effectiveness of Scrum'.

Scrum Assessments & Credentials

At present, there are two popular organizations providing different *types* and *levels* of *role-based* Scrum credentials: **Scrum Alliance**, and **Scrum.org**. See Tables 1.1 and 1.2. The **CSM** credential is the most popular today, but acceptance of the **PSM** credentials is rapidly growing.

The **Project Management Institute (PMI)** also offers the ***PMI Agile Certified Practitioner (PMI-ACP)***, which: (a) extends beyond Scrum, to cover other Agile methodologies, (b) extends beyond a specific role (e.g. Scrum Master), to cover facets of other roles as 'Practitioner', and (c) leans toward the 'project management' aspects of Agile projects. Due to significant awareness and influence of PMI, the PMI-ACP credential is also getting very popular and acceptance amongst many companies, particularly those, which already *desire* or *require* the **Project Management Professional (PMP)** credential to participate in their projects. *Since this book series focuses only on Scrum and Scrum Master Certification, it will not address the PMI-ACP assessment, content, or credential.*

In case of *Scrum Alliance*, there is a Certification for each of the three Scrum roles: *Scrum Master*, *Product Owner*, and *Developer*. After achieving any of these credentials, one can attain the CSP credential to designate an advanced knowledge and experience in Scrum.

Table 1.1: Scrum Alliance Credentials

Role	Credential
1. **Fundamental**	
Scrum Master	**Certified Scrum Master (CSM)**
Product Owner	Certified Scrum Product Owner (CSPO)
Developer	Certified Scrum Developer (CSD)
2. **Advanced**	
Professional	**Certified Scrum Professional (CSP)**
Trainer	Certified Scrum Trainer (CST)
Coach	Certified Scrum Coach (CSC)

Those who wish to become a trainer or coach may plan to obtain the CST/CSC credentials; particularly, if they plan to offer training courses certified by Scrum Alliance.

Figure 1.1: Scrum Alliance Certification Path

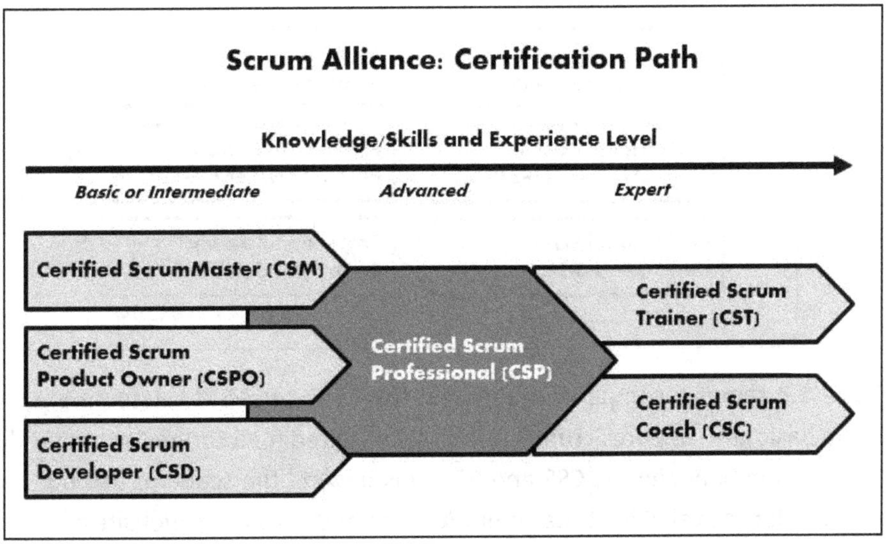

On the other hand, in case of Scrum.org, there are two levels of Certification for each of the three Scrum roles – Level I and Level II.

Table 1.2: Scrum.org Credentials

Role	Credential
1. Fundamental	
Scrum Master	Professional Scrum Master Level I (PSM I)
Product Owner	Professional Scrum Product Owner Level I (PSPO I)
Developer	Professional Scrum Developer Level I (PSD I)
2. Advanced	
Scrum Master	Professional Scrum Master Level II (PSM II)
Product Owner	Professional Scrum Product Owner Level II (PSPO II)
Developer	*Professional Scrum Developer Level II (PSD II)*

Professional Scrum Developer Level II certification is not yet available.

Figure 1.2: Scrum.Org Certification Path

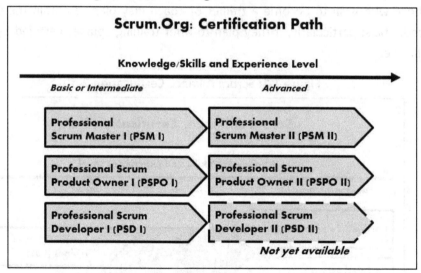

Table 1.3 shows a comparison between the CSM and PSM I Assessments, which test a basic level of Core Scrum knowledge, required for a Scrum Master credential. Comparison between the CSP and PSM II is beyond the scope of this book series; information is available at the Scrum Alliance and Scrum.org websites:

CSM: https://www.scrumalliance.org/certifications/practitioners/certified-scrummaster-csm

CSP: https://www.scrumalliance.org/certifications/practitioners/csp-certification

PSM I: https://www.scrum.org/Assessments/Professional-Scrum-Master-Assessments/PSM-I-Assessment

PSM II: https://www.scrum.org/Assessments/Professional-Scrum-Master-Assessments/PSM-II-Assessment

Table 1.3: Scrum Master Assessments Compared

Parameter	CSM	PSM-I
Courses (Pre-requisite)	Certified ScrumMaster course from CST	None
Available Courses	Several (from official REP and unofficial providers)	*Professional Scrum Foundations*, or *Professional Scrum Master*
Test Fee	$25/attempt (1st 2 attempts free)	$100/attempt
Number of Questions	35	80
Passing Score	Approx. 70% (i.e. 24 of 35)	85%
Time Limit	**Unlimited** but plan for an hour or so (to be taken within 90 days of completing the CSM course).	60 minutes
Format	Multiple Choices (Single-Response), True/False	Multiple Choices (Single-/Multiple Response), True/False
Practice Assessment	None	Scrum Open
Study Topics	CSM Subject Areas: • General Knowledge • Scrum Roles • Scrum Meetings • Scrum Artifacts	PSM I Subject Areas • Scrum Framework • Scrum Theory & Principles • Cross-functional, self-organizing Teams • Coaching & Facilitation
Primary Resource	Core Scrum	The Scrum Guide

Links to Key Resources:

Core Scrum (CSM):

> https://www.scrumalliance.org/why-scrum/core-scrum-values-roles

Scrum Guide (PSM I) – also useful for CSM:

> http://www.scrumguides.org/docs/scrumguide/v1/scrum-guide-us.pdf

Scrum Open (PSM I) – also useful for CSM – is a *free* **online practice assessment**, which the CSM/PSM aspirant must **master** before taking the actual assessment (i.e. repeatedly take the assessment until you get 100% score, at least 3 or 4 consecutive times):

> https://www.scrum.org/Assessments/Open-Assessments/Scrum-Open-Assessment

OPTIONAL: **Scrum Practitioner Open** (PSM I) – also useful for CSM – is a *free* **online practice assessment**, which is more relevant to the **Scaled Scrum** subject area. This area is usually excluded from the scope of CSM/PSM I assessments; however, the Scrum Master candidate could attempt this assessment to be more familiar with few 'gray areas' of Scrum:

> https://www.scrum.org/Assessments/Open-Assessments/Scrum-Practitioner-Open-Assessment

Personally, for the purpose of attaining the CSM/PSM I credentials, I would not advise the candidate to read any article or book, or use any resource other than those listed above, in addition to any CSM, PSM, or PSF course you may take.

Purpose

The only purpose of this book series is to provide a *focused approach* to help achieve the audience's *focused objective*: *attain **Scrum Master** Credential at the minimum cost and time*. It does not seek to provide an *adequate* background on *Agile* methodologies, or a complete description of *Scrum* principles and practices. The focus is on providing *just as much information is required; just in time*.

This book series has been developed primarily from my own experience, taking into account what was most important while preparing for the assessments, as well as while actually taking the assessments. A continual endeavor will be made to enhance to coverage and effectiveness of the content.

While this book series is aimed at those interested in Scrum Master Certification, it will be useful for other certification aspirants – Product Owners, Developers – since it provides quite an *extensive* coverage of **Scrum Fundamentals**, common to these roles.

Audience & Certification Roadmap

While, the target audience is primarily an aspirant of Scrum Master Certification, each book in this series has a specific focus depending on the candidate's objective and background, particularly, in terms of knowledge and experience.

Figure 1.3: Study and Certification Path

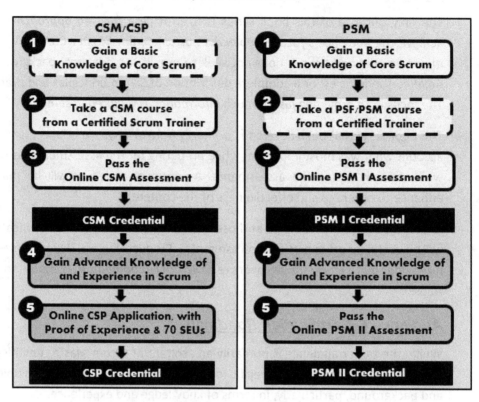

Figure 1.4: How These Books Fit into the Path

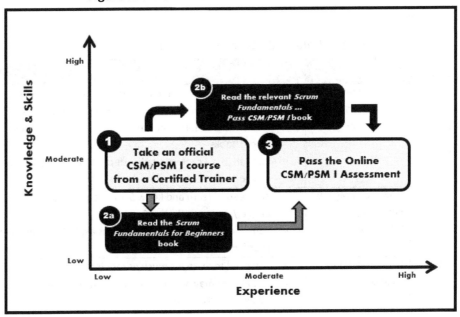

A candidate can, potentially, have one or more combination of the following objectives.

Table 1.4: Potential Objectives of Scrum Master Aspirants

TYPE	OBJECTIVE	REQUIREMENT
A	I wish to **learn** as much as possible about Scrum	• You do not need to practice Scrum or get a credential • You can learn on your own using various free and paid resources available over the Internet, and buying a few 'good' books • You can join a professionally offered training program or course
B	I wish to **apply** my knowledge of Scrum (**practice** Scrum)	• You need to learn and know Scrum; and join a project/team, which uses Scrum • You do not need a credential, unless explicitly required by your 'employer'
C	I wish to attain a valid **credential** in Scrum	• You need to learn '*as much as required*' • You may or may not need to take an **official** professionally administered course.

Scrum Experts recommend you fulfill the above objectives in the following order: A, B, C

The target audience of this book series comprises candidates with Objective C. Nonetheless, other candidates (with Objectives A and B) may find this book series useful. Typically, the candidate *learns 'as much as is required'* to **pass the assessment in the first attempt**, and *within a week of self-study*.

Another criterion that needs to be taken into account is the candidate's own background (or profile) i.e. the degree of knowledge and experience the candidate already possesses.

As stated above, most Scrum experts recommend that candidates should acquire a credential after 'sufficient' *knowledge* of Scrum and *experience* in the Industry. However, this is more often a stated norm than a requirement.

If both knowledge as well as experience were required, the accreditation agency would have specified the minimum requirements. In the absence of such constraints, the following recommendations may be made.

Table 1.5: Select Profiles of Scrum Master Aspirants

TYPE	PROFILE	RECOMMENDATION
A	Little or no knowledge and experience of Scrum	• You can learn on your own using various free and paid resources available over the Internet, and buying a few 'good' books • You should consider joining a professionally offered training program or course
B	Moderate knowledge but Little or no experience of Scrum	• You may consider joining a professionally offered training program or course • You need join a project/team, which uses Scrum • You may consider attaining a credential
C	Moderate knowledge and experience of Scrum	• You need to learn *as much as required* • You may or may not need to take an **official** professionally administered course. • You should consider attaining a credential

This Book Series is primarily targeted at Scrum Master aspirants with the above profile or background. Nonetheless, those with more knowledge and/or experience would find one or more of these books helpful in attaining the Scrum Master Certification.

Candidates **with little or no knowledge and experience** in Scrum are expected to **pass the Scrum Master assessment within one month** of preparation using the 'Scrum Fundamentals for Beginners'.

Other candidates are expected to pass the assessment within one week of preparation using the relevant guidebook in this series.

Table 1.6: Recommended Book for Each Candidate Profile

BOOK IN THE SERIES	PROFILE	NOTES
1. Scrum Fundamentals for ScrumAlliance Certified ScrumMaster Certification: Pass the CSM assessment in One Week	B, C	For those who wish to take the **CSM Assessment only**
2. Scrum Fundamentals for Scrum.org Professional Scrum Master I Certification: Pass the PSM I assessment in One Week	B, C	For those who wish to take the **PSM I Assessment only**
3. Scrum Fundamentals for Scrum Master Certification: Pass the CSM/PSM I assessments in One Week	B, C	For those who wish to take the **CSM and PSM I Assessments**
4. Scrum Fundamentals for Beginners: Pass the CSM/PSM I assessments in One Month	A	For those who wish to take the **CSM and/or PSM I Assessments**

Each of these books in this series is highly focused on the candidate's objective of *minimizing time and costs* and *maximizing value or return on investment* (i.e. success in passing the Assessment).

Organization

Each of the books is organized in a similar fashion, starting with a common **Introduction**. The same *Introduction* in each book ensures that each Reader gets a similar overview of relevant content, regardless of which book he or she bought. For instance, a CSM candidate gets an adequate exposure to the PSM certification, even if he or she is interested only in the CSM certification at present. Each book contains a '*Roadmap to Certification*' section, which provides alternative '*pathways*' to different credentials, depending on the candidate profile and 'tools' to be used.

The next part, **Scrum Certification**, provides details on how to attain and maintain the credential: accrediting agency, credential, pre-requisites, application process, professionally administered courses, assessment scope, assessment and certification process, to name a few

The third part, *Strategy*, provides details on developing a sound, personal 'Preparation Strategy' as well as a 'Test Strategy' to achieve the candidate's goals/objectives.

In *Part 4: Scrum Fundamentals*, we shall go through several examples so that you can make the appropriate judgment. This is the main part of the book, which discusses the various aspects of Scrum as required to be covered in the Assessment

Table 1.7: Assessment Section or Subject Area

#	CSM	PSM I
1.	General Knowledge	Scrum Framework
2.	Scrum Roles	Scrum Theory & Principles
3.	Scrum Meetings	Cross-functional, Self-organizing Teams
4.	Scrum Artifacts	Coaching & Facilitation

Part 2: Scrum Certification

The CSM Course

To attain the **Certified ScrumMaster (CSM)** credentials of *Scrum Alliance*, you are required to attend an *official* **2-day CSM course**, provided by a *Registered Education Provider (REP)*, and conducted by a *Certified Scrum Trainer (CST)*. I was very fortunate to attend a CSM training course conducted by *Jeff McKenna*, one of the *founding fathers* of Scrum.

At the end of the two-day CSM course, the trainer certifies that you have completed the course. Jeff, in his typical half-humorous, half-serious way, pointed out that you have to be 'physically and mentally present for almost all of the two days', before the Trainer can certify this. S/he then hands you a **signed certificate** *after successful completion of the course*, towards the end of the second day.

Later that day (or perhaps, the next), you get a '**Welcome email**' from Scrum Alliance providing the *login* for *your Scrum Alliance account*. You first set up the password once you receive this email; then log in to your account and prepare yourself to take the **Online Test** at the '*CSM Test Site'*.

The CSM Test

Your *CSM test fee* is already included in the price of the CSM course you have completed. Per present policy, you can take the test twice (only if you fail in the first attempt) without any payment, within 90 days. After up to two attempts, there's a $25 charge for each additional attempt. *Scrum Alliance* does not yet specify the *maximum* number of attempts, or *maximum* timeframe by which you must pass this test after completion of the course.

<u>You can 'start, stop and restart' this test anytime, and any number of times.</u>

To get a passing score, you must **correctly answer 24 of the 35 questions** (approximately, 70%), even though you will see later that the *Scrum Alliance* states that a score of 66% or more is required to pass the test.

After you pass the CSM test, you will be asked to accept the License Agreement and complete your Scrum Alliance membership profile.

The CSM Test Score Report

Once you complete and submit the test, your score report will be almost instantly generated (of course, this depends on your internet connection).

Figure 2.1: CSM Test Report - Overall

My Account History and Content Taken Detail

Completed - Take a Test

You are finished taking the following test:

Name	Certified Scrum Master (CSM) Test - FirstAttempt
Date:	June 06, 2010 2:06:17 AM EDT
Taken By	jdoe1

Thank you for completing the Certified ScrumMaster® test. Congratulations on a job well done – you passed!

Now return to your Scrum Alliance profile at www.scrumalliance.org to accept the License Agreement, complete your membership contact information, print your Certified ScrumMaster certificate, and complete your public profile. You can return to these test details at any time through a link next to your test score in your profile. This information is kept private for you.

Your certification is valid for two years. You will then need to renew by meeting recertification guidelines.

Your Scrum Alliance profile can be kept public to market your new certification and skills or can be made private. To manage these settings, access your dashboard by logging into your account and clicking on the link located at the top right corner of the screen. Then choose the settings that best meet your career and community needs.

 If you have any questions or issues, contact us at support@scrumalliance.org

Score	**PASS**
	35 points scored (or 100.0%) out of 35 maximum points
	(a score of 66.0% or greater is needed to pass this test)

Figure 2.2: CSM Test Report - Scores

Summary of Results By Section

The questions in this test were organized by section. This table details a summary of your scores by section.

Section/Subject Area	Question Count	Points Available	Points Scored	Percentage Scored
CSM General Knowledge	7	7	7	100.00%
CSM Scrum Roles	20	20	20	100.00%
CSM Scrum Meetings	4	4	4	100.00%
CSM Scrum Artifacts	4	4	4	100.00%

In case you were not able to get the perfect score, the Report will include an assessment of all the questions you were not able to answer correctly. This will include the response you selected, as well as the correct answer.

Figure 2.3: Assessment of Incorrect Responses

3)	Which technique is a productive method for the ScrumMaster to use to help facilitate communication between the Team and Product Owner?	Value	Score
	Choose the best answer.		
	A) ○ Teach the Product Owner about the technologies employed during the Sprints.	0	0
	B) ○ Teach the Team to talk in terms of business needs and objectives.	0	0
✗	C) ◉ Facilitate collaborative meetings between them.	0	0
–	D) ○ All of these	1	0

Incorrect: Your answer is incorrect. 0 points.

The Following Answer Is Incorrect

Facilitate collaborative meetings between them.

Once you have passed the CSM assessment, there are several activities you need to complete:

- Set up your Profile
- Generate and download your certificate
- Maintain your credentials, etc.

Detailed information is available at:

http://www.scrumalliance.org/certifications/practitioners/certified-scrummaster-(csm)/becoming-a-certified-scrummaster

The CSM Test Coverage

The questions on the CSM test are based on the **CSM Content Outline Learning Objectives** established for the CSM course.

Please see details at:

https://www.scrumalliance.org/scrum/media/ScrumAllianceMedia/Files%20and%20PDFs/Certifications/CSM/CSM-Content-Outline-Learning-Objectives.pdf

Part 3: Strategy

Preparing for the Assessment

There's a widespread myth that *'the more you study, the more you learn'*. On the contrary, you may actually land up knowing less, or more confused.

Scrum today does not have an official 'body of knowledge', by design. Scrum proponents do not believe in formalism and rigid borders; as a result, Scrum is envisaged as a Framework, which allows for a high degree of flexibility. The only formal specification of Scrum is in **The Scrum Guide**, authored by *Ken Schwaber* and *Jeff Sutherland*. This is the guide, which Scrum.org follows in letter and spirit.

The adoption of Scrum, per Scrum.org, is highly constrained by the rules of Scrum as laid down in the Scrum Guide. Any implementation of Scrum, which does not follow the rules of Scrum, is not considered Scrum by Scrum.org. It's considered *Scrum-like...*, *Scrum-but...*, but definitely, not Scrum.

Figure 3.1: Core Scrum Framework – Scrum.org

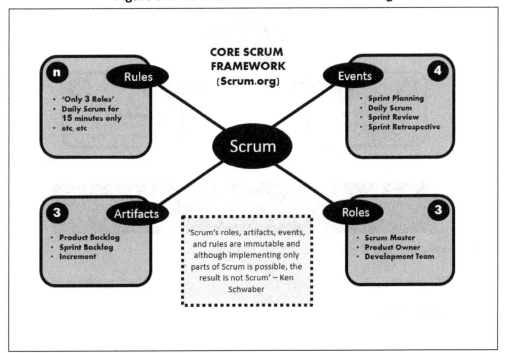

On the other hand, the Scrum Alliance is slightly more flexible about what Scrum really is. In other words, the Scrum Alliance is not very rigid about the Scrum rules; and has now modified Scrum to include practices adopted by Scrum, which were originally not in Scrum. As a result, there is some divergence between the Scrum specifications championed by Scrum.org and the Scrum Alliance. The latter has now come out with its own specification of Scrum in the form of a guide called the **Core Scrum**.

Figure 3.2: Core Scrum Framework – Scrum Alliance

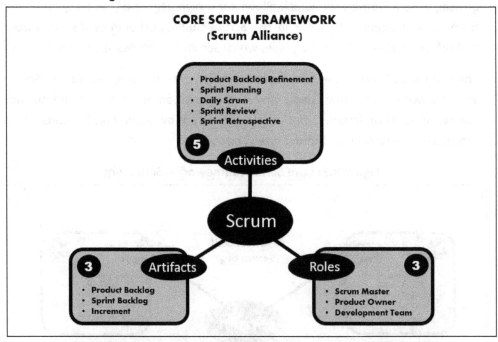

To prepare for the CSM assessment, start with The Scrum Guide and follow up with Core Scrum

Scrum Guide (PSM I) – also useful for CSM:

http://www.scrumguides.org/docs/scrumguide/v1/scrum-guide-us.pdf

Core Scrum (CSM):

https://www.scrumalliance.org/why-scrum/core-scrum-values-roles

It is extremely important to understand the:

- fundamentals of Scrum, and
- differences in the specifications of Scrum, as laid down in these two guides

I recommend that you read these two guides over and over again, until you have understood the philosophy behind the framework, its core values and principles. This will help you a lot during the assessment while responding to questions, which are either not straightforward or even perhaps somewhat misleading.

Since you have to take the CSM course, I will not recommend any other study material or text book if your objective is *just to pass the CSM assessment*.

While it may appear that it will help you gain more knowledge if you were to read a variety of books or articles (e.g. suggested reading, as recommended on Scrum.org or Scrum Alliance sites), this may actually lead to *information overload* (due to too much information), or *total confusion* (due to conflicting information). There are several aspects on which even Scrum Experts disagree.

> **Any source of information that precedes The Scrum Guide of July 2013 should be discarded.**

The July 2013 version of The Scrum Guide continues to be the best source of information on Scrum. The other best source is the Scrum Alliance Core Scrum v2014.08.15.

Any text or study material, which refers to an earlier version of the Scrum Guide should be completely discarded, since significant changes in the Scrum framework were incorporated in this version. Any text or reference material, which makes a mention of chickens and pigs, or refers to the Sprint Review as a mere Demo, should also be discarded. You may need to look an updated version of such books or reference materials.

The best approach for Test Prep is summarized below:

1. Complete the CSM Course
2. Before you start studying for the assessment, take the Scrum Open:

   https://www.scrum.org/Assessments/Open-Assessments/Scrum-Open-Assessment

3. Record the 'No-Prep, Baseline Score' you obtained
4. Read The Scrum Guide & Core Scrum
5. Read the relevant Scrum Fundamentals book, which is suitable for your profile
6. Go to Step 2, until you are ready to go to Step 7
7. Take the CSM Assessment and pass it.

Figure 3.3: CSM Test Prep Strategy

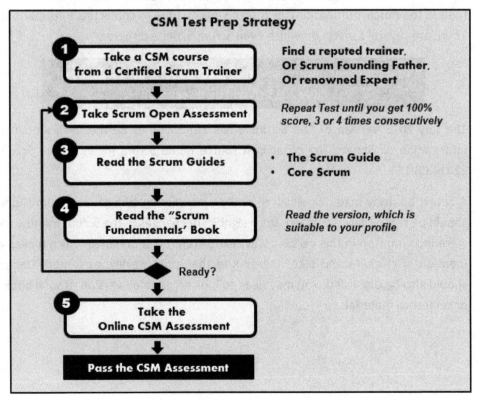

Figure 3.4: CSM Test Prep Strategy based on Profile

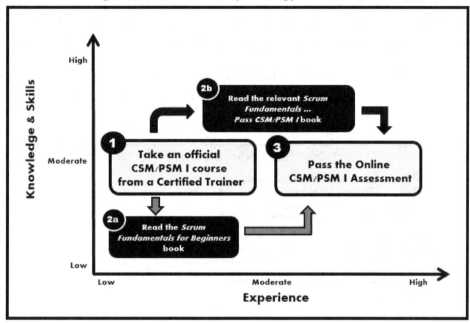

Table 3.1: Recommended Book for Each Candidate Profile

BOOK IN THE SERIES	PROFILE	NOTES
1. Scrum Fundamentals for ScrumAlliance Certified ScrumMaster Certification: Pass the CSM assessment in One Week	B, C	For those who wish to take the **CSM Assessment only**
2. Scrum Fundamentals for Scrum.org Professional Scrum Master I Certification: Pass the PSM I assessment in One Week	B, C	For those who wish to take the **PSM I Assessment only**
3. Scrum Fundamentals for Scrum Master Certification: Pass the CSM/PSM I assessments in One Week	B, C	For those who wish to take the **CSM and PSM I Assessments**
4. Scrum Fundamentals for Beginners: Pass the CSM/PSM I assessments in One Month	A	For those who wish to take the **CSM and/or PSM I Assessments**

Taking the Assessment

It may be no understatement when I say that the CSM Assessment is, perhaps, the easiest test you would have taken in your life. There are two reasons I state this:

- Its coverage is limited to the core concepts of Scrum
- There is practically no time limit for the test, even after you have started it

Figure 3.5: CSM Test Taking Strategy

CSM Test Taking Strategy

1. Take a CSM course from a Certified Scrum Trainer
2. Take Scrum Open Assessment
3. Read the Scrum Guides
4. Read the "Scrum Fundamentals' Book

Ready?

5. Take the Online CSM Assessment

- *Take time to understand the question, and the responses*
- *Take time to reject incorrect responses*
- *Take time to select correct responses*

Pass the CSM Assessment

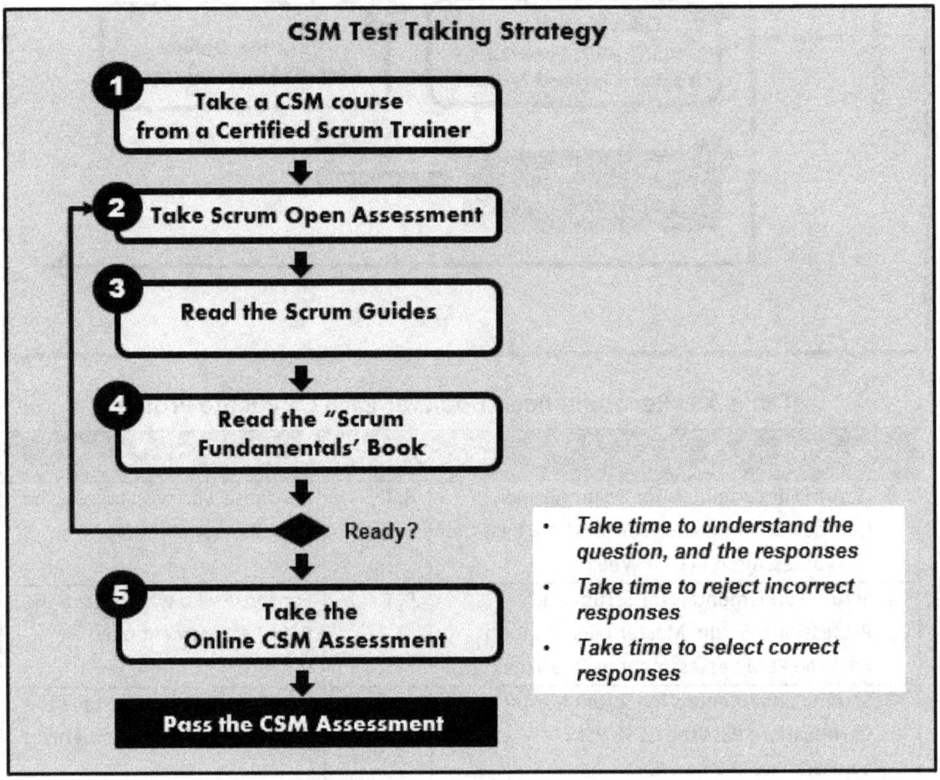

The most important aspect about Scrum Assessments to consider is the occasional subjectivity of a response or response set.

Very often, there are responses, which border on the 'gray area'; and, it become extremely difficult to select or reject an option. This is particularly so when leading and renowned experts agree to disagree. Scrum demands flexibility as opposed to rigidity and determinism. On the other hand, few experts are quite dogmatic in their beliefs and are opposed to change and adaption. This is quite paradoxical. Nonetheless, you are advised to rule out the most obviously incorrect options, and select one of the best remaining options – based on your concrete knowledge as well as your understanding of the Scrum philosophy, principles and values.

Before developing these strategies, a few **determining factors** will need to be analyzed and understood. For instance, the candidate needs to develop a keen ability to <u>distinguish between the *'objective type'* of questions, vis-à-vis the *'subjective type'*.</u> By these, I do not refer to questions with *'single-choice'* or *'multiple-choice'* responses. Instead, I'm referring to the **SUBJECTIVITY** of the *question and/or 'correct response/s'* as determined by the test author.

Consider the following example:

1) Which of the following is the best color?

(A) Red
(B) Blue
(C) Yellow
(D) Green

It's immaterial whether you are asked to select <u>one</u> or <u>more than one</u> correct *response*. The ***degree of subjectivity*** appears reduced when you are asked to select the *'best answer'* instead of the *'correct answer'*.

Consider the above example again, with the question slightly rephrased:

2) Which of the following, in your mind, is the best color?

(A) Red
(B) Blue
(C) Yellow
(D) Green

The situation doesn't really change. You are as unsure as you were while dealing with Q1. You simply don't know what the test author thought was the correct/best response.

The above examples illustrate the *highest* degree of subjectivity and ambiguity. Thankfully, real-life subjective questions may not be as ambiguous (except, perhaps, in psychological testing).

Now consider a 'real life' example below:

3) The Development Team should not be interrupted during the Sprint. The Sprint Goal should remain intact. These are conditions that foster creativity, quality and productivity. Based on this, which of the following is FALSE?

A) The Product Owner can help clarify or optimize the Sprint when asked by the Development Team.

B) The Sprint Backlog and its contents are fully formulated in the Sprint Planning meeting and do not change during the Sprint.

C) As a decomposition of the selected Product Backlog Items, the Sprint Backlog changes and may grow as the work emerges.

D) The Development Team may work with the Product Owner to remove or add work if it finds it has more or less capacity than it expected.

Very often, the **best answer is selected by an iterative process of elimination**: *eliminating choices, which you know are obviously false, one after the other.*

First of all, pay ***special attention*** to this type of question where you have to **identify one or more FALSE responses**; i.e. you have to eliminate the correct answer choice/s. In examples similar to the above, a check box or radio button will indicate where you are expected to select only one or more than one response/s. In this example, there is only one choice to be made i.e. only one option is false. Can you determine the correct answer for Example 3? It is Option (B).

Part 4: Scrum Fundamentals

Chapter 1: General Knowledge

Brief History of Scrum

The term **Scrum** was *borrowed* from the game of rugby, wherein Scrum (short for 'scrummage') is a method for restarting play, either after a minor infraction or if the ball has gone out of play.

Jeff Sutherland, *Jeff McKenna* and *John Scumniotales* created the Scrum methodology and started the very first Scrum team at *Easel Corporation* in 1993. They were the first to use the term *Scrum*, and were influenced by the reference to the approach described by *Hirotaka Takeuchi* and *Ikujiro Nonaka*, in their 1986 paper published in *Harvard Business Review – 'The New New Product Development Game'*:

http://hbr.org/1986/01/the-new-new-product-development-game/ar/1

Since the early 1990s, **Ken Schwaber** had been using a similar approach, which would later become Scrum at his company, *Advanced Development Methods*.

The term and approach became formalized after **Schwaber** and **Sutherland** co-presented a paper on Scrum at the OOPSLA Conference in Austin, Texas, in 1995. Since then, they have collaborated very closely to develop the Scrum *body of knowledge*. They have co-authored **The Scrum Guide**, the official, de-facto *bible* for Scrum practitioners worldwide.

Ken Schwaber is responsible for founding the **Scrum Alliance** and creating the **Certified Scrum Master** programs and its derivatives. He left the Scrum Alliance in the fall of 2009 and then founded **Scrum.org** to improve the quality and effectiveness of Scrum.

The Agile Manifesto

Various Agile Methodologies are guided by the *Agile Manifesto*, which was written in February 2001, by 17 ''independent-minded practitioners of several programming methodologies'', at a summit held at Snowbird in Utah.

Figure 4.1.1: The Agile Manifesto

Manifesto for Agile Software Development

We are uncovering better ways of developing
software by doing it and helping others do it.
Through this work we have come to value:

Individuals and interactions over *processes and tools*
Working software over *comprehensive documentation*
Customer collaboration over *contract negotiation*
Responding to change over *following a plan*

That is, while there is value in the items on
the right, we value the items on the left more.

More details are available at:

http://www.agilemanifesto.org/

http://www.agilealliance.org/the-alliance/the-agile-manifesto/

The 17 original signatories included Kent Beck, Mike Beedle, Arie van Bennekum, Alistair Cockburn, Ward Cunningham, Martin Fowler, James Grenning, Jim Highsmith, Andrew Hunt, Ron Jeffries, Jon Kern, Brian Marick, Steve Mellor, Ken Schwaber, Jeff Sutherland, and Dave Thomas. More information on their background and contributions is available at:

http://www.agilemanifesto.org/authors.html

Per the Scrum manifesto, Scrum entails constantly evolving or improving ways to produce better software, through a process of discovery based on the concepts of transparency, inspection and adaption.

In the traditional world, there is a major focus on standardization of process and compliance; and achieving efficiency through the use of common tools, techniques and templates. **In the Scrum world, the focus is primarily on the people and how they interact**. Processes and tools, while important, become a secondary consideration. Empowerment of the people in the team is a primary objective. They get to decide how much work to do and how to do it, based on their assessment of the team's productivity. People in the team self-organize and manage the work by themselves.

This is a strict contrast to the traditional way, where people are managed and directed by the management e.g. a Team Lead, Project Manager, or IT Manager. The team is assigned a scope of work along with a deadline, even if the team was involved in the assessments to determine the scope or effort required.

Under the traditional model, there is a clearly laid-out sequence of activities, in *Phases*, with specified *Gates* or *Milestones*. During each Phase, the team is required to produce several mandatory and optional artifacts. For instance, the ***Software or Product Development Lifecycle*** in an organization may have a Phase called ***'Requirements Gathering and Analysis'***. This begins after business stakeholders deliver a *Vision Statement* and a *Project Charter* at a *'Business Commit'* gate. During this phase, *Business Analysts* are required to produce and deliver a ***Business Requirements Document (BRD)***. Additionally, there could be a report on *'Cross-functional Technical/Functional Impact Analysis'* or a *'Business or Technical Feasibility Report'*, which preceded the BRD or was developed simultaneously. In short, there are many forms to fill out, and many templates to fill in to produce a number of artifacts.

In the Scrum world, the focus changes to a working software with documentation kept to the bare minimum. People mistakenly believe that minimum means zero. This is not correct. There may be quite a few documents developed during the Sprints. Please see the section on ***Definition of Done*** in subsequent pages.

In various organizations, quite intuitively, there is a lot of time spent on resource management, funding and cost management. Several workers and managers continuously work on the Budget and Spend, under a high degree of management oversight. Contract and vendor management is a key area of focus. Reconciliation of costs or spend to budgets becomes a very serious and complex exercise, particularly when there is a complex mix of *fixed-price* and *time-and-materials* cost based projects.

This problem becomes quite simplified when teams implement Scrum. Firstly, the Scrum team comprises 5-11 team members who are, more or less, permanently allocated to the team and perhaps, at the same location. The cost of maintaining this team is fairly constant and can be easily determined. Finally, any wastage or 'loss' can be contained to some degree of 'minimum'. In other words, the extent of loss could be cost of the work completed in two Sprints, if the entire work if 'throw-away'. In contrast, wastage or loss under the traditional model is either difficult to identify/compute, or is determined too late in the cycle to allow for any meaningful correction.

As a result, there is more transparency and visibility, particularly, of cost and progress to the customer. This results in higher trust and thereby, greater collaboration and continued engagement.

Finally, Scrum encourages changes. Under the traditional model, managers often frown upon changes because they believe these changes introduces risks to their 'perfectly' crafted plans. Even if changes are reviewed and accepted, which is more an exception than norm, these are implemented after a fairly long development cycle. Of course, there are exceptions when changes are made fairly quickly; but, these are determined by priority and business justification. For instance, if there is an issue in the Production environment which inhibits customers from placing an order easily, this issue will be dealt with very promptly – in a matter of days, if not hours. However, we are concerned with Change as a constant phenomenon.

As a corollary, Planning also becomes less 'important'. No one is interested in building a detailed and perfect plan. On the other hand, planning starts with only the information at hand. The plan constantly evolves as and when more information becomes available. Planning and execution i.e. work is primarily determined by experience and experimentation, under an empirical process like Scrum.

More details are available at:

http://www.agilealliance.org/the-alliance/the-agile-manifesto/

Aside from the Agile Manifesto, another key element of Scrum is the 'Twelve Principles of Scrum'. It would be an understatement to state that this is perhaps the most important element required in order to understand and implement Scrum.

These principles determine whether Scrum has been adequately understood and applied. Very often, this requires a complete change in the organization culture; and particularly, how the team or manager perform their duties.

As opposed to team being managed or directed by Managers, the Scrum team is self-organizing. Management is never involved in the day-to-day operations of the team. More details are provided in subsequent sections to elaborate on these concepts.

Figure 4.1.2: The Twelve Principles of Agile Software

Principles behind the Agile Manifesto

We follow these principles:

Our highest priority is to satisfy the customer
through early and continuous delivery
of valuable software.

Welcome changing requirements, even late in
development. Agile processes harness change for
the customer's competitive advantage.

Deliver working software frequently, from a
couple of weeks to a couple of months, with a
preference to the shorter timescale.

Business people and developers must work
together daily throughout the project.

Build projects around motivated individuals.
Give them the environment and support they need,
and trust them to get the job done.

The most efficient and effective method of
conveying information to and within a development
team is face-to-face conversation.

Working software is the primary measure of progress.

Agile processes promote sustainable development.
The sponsors, developers, and users should be able
to maintain a constant pace indefinitely.

Continuous attention to technical excellence
and good design enhances agility.

Simplicity--the art of maximizing the amount
of work not done--is essential.

The best architectures, requirements, and designs
emerge from self-organizing teams.

At regular intervals, the team reflects on how
to become more effective, then tunes and adjusts
its behavior accordingly

Scrum Foundations

Empirical and defined processes

The Scrum Framework is based on **empirical** process control model, as opposed to a **defined** process control model.

Firstly, in an *empirical* model, there is less reliance on *planning*; and more reliance on *experimentation*, *observation*, and *experience*. Instead of detailed plans based on well specified scope, or detailed requirements, work begins with any or sketchy information available. Knowledge comes from experience and decisions are based on what is known at that time. The 'details' are built up through incremental iterations over a period of time.

On the other hand, in a *defined* model, there is a mandatory need to discover the details as much as possible before a subsequent action can happen. For instance, the requirements needs to be 'completely' defined, before a 'fool-proof' plan can be developed, and stakeholders sign off on the scope. Architecture, Design and Development starts after Requirements are 'defined and frozen'.

Secondly, the concept of *Monitoring* and *Control* is very different in the case of empirical models. There is no '*hard-and-fast* **baseline**' against which deviation is to be monitored and controlled. Instead, there is an implicit assumption that the team does not know what is the *most optimal* **time** or **cost** or **effort** associated with a particular task or feature. Based on experience and knowledge gathered over a period of time, the team will discover some degree of it; and this will be applied in future iterations. To facilitate this, the team **inspects** and **adapts** to changing needs and situations very often, through well-defined checkpoint mechanisms, to improve the quality of the task as well as the output. To make this *control* effective, the team must be empowered and self-organizing, with very little management intervention from outside the team. This requires an organizational culture marked by **transparency**, **trust** and **competence**.

Finally, the empirical model works best in case of **complex** environments or systems, where *ambiguity* is inherent as the norm rather than as an exception. In such cases, it is more appropriate and meaningful to tackle smaller problems and assess results in a shorter period of time and adapt accordingly, rather than spend too much time decomposing the ambiguity to arrive at a perfect plan to move a mountain.

Question 4.1.1: Upon what type of process control is Scrum based?

A) Empirical
B) Hybrid
C) Defined
D) Complex

Transparency, Inspection and Adaptation are the three pillars of Scrum

At any point in time, there should be complete transparency with respect to the work as well as the outputs. Status of work-in-progress or completed should be clearly visible to the Scrum team, as well as any interested stakeholder outside the team. The quality of the output or artifacts should also be determined and improved through continual *formal* and *informal* inspections and adaptation to suggested improvements. Informal inspections may be conducted, without being intrusive or disruptive, during the development cycle; while formal inspections are more or less mandated during pre-defined checkpoints.

Question 4.1.2: The three pillars of empirical process control are:

A) Respect For People, Kaizen, Eliminating Waste
B) Planning, Demonstration, Retrospective
C) Inspection, Transparency, Adaptation
D) Planning, Inspection, Adaptation
E) Transparency, Eliminating Waste, Kaizen

Q4.1.3: What does it mean to say that an event has a timebox?

A) The event must happen at a set time.
B) The event must happen by a given time.
C) The event must take at least a minimum amount of time.
D) The event can take no more than a maximum amount of time.

Frequent *informal* inspections allow for timely detection and correction of issues well before the formal events. Also, it will alleviate the need of detailed inspections at formal checkpoints, which make them less effective. Nonetheless, the frequency and scope of these inspections should not be that high that the desired progress of development work is impeded.

Figure 4.1.3: The Three Pillars of Scrum

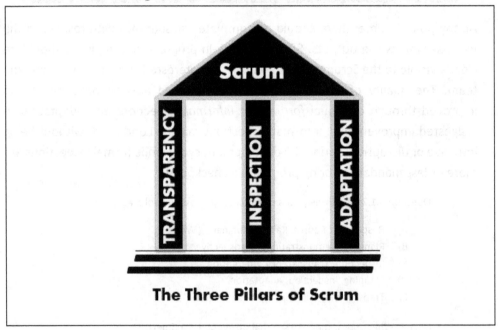

Scrum prescribes four formal events for inspection and adaptation:

- Sprint Planning
- Daily Scrum
- Sprint Review
- Sprint Retrospective

Sprint

Scrum uses *iterative* and **incremental** development cycle, known as the Sprint. It is **timeboxed** and **protected**.

The fundamental rules of Scrum dictate that each Sprint should be time-boxed, and the Sprint duration should be constant across various sprints. **A timebox determines that maximum time allowed for the event**; and, once it is set, under no circumstances, should it be exceeded.

Typically, the duration of a Sprint is one of the following:

- One Week
- Two Weeks
- Four Weeks (i.e. One Month)

A Sprint duration of either *One Week*, or *Two Weeks*, is most common.

It is rare for Sprints to be of either of the following durations: *Three Weeks*, or *More than a Month* (Most experts consider a Sprint duration of more than a month to be unacceptable). **The next sprint starts as soon as the previous one ends**. Very often, the Sprint is selected to start on a Tuesday or Wednesday (instead of Mondays or Fridays). A *shorter* Sprint Duration is generally considered as *better*.

Sometimes, some expert recommend starting with a 2-week Sprint during early adoption of Scrum, and then later switching to a 1-week Sprint on gaining some maturity. This is considered a classic case of experimentation and adaptation.

Sprint Zero (or Sprint 0)

The concept of Sprint Zero is very controversial amongst various Scrum proponents. Some consider it a helpful transition from a previous practice. Others consider that it's an artificial concept to explain activities undertaken prior to a Sprint. According to Ken Schwaber, "Sprint 0 has become a phrase misused to describe the planning that occurs prior to the first sprint".

Proponents of Sprint Zero consider it the Sprint required for initial prep work e.g. assembling the team, setting up the infrastructure, preparing the Product Backlog, some high-level design or architecture work, etc. Very often, the duration of this Sprint is longer. For instance, if the regular sprint is 2-week long, Sprint 0 may last for 4 weeks.

Opponents consider this as an unnecessary distinction. They believe that these activities are undertaken in parallel or in increments during the Sprint. Sprint Planning and Backlog grooming are part of the Sprint. Environment setup is usually undertaken by a different team, and the infrastructure is available at the beginning of the Sprint.

Sprint Zero is not an officially sanctioned event in Scrum; and may be considered an extension, like several others (pl. see Appendix 1), which may be adopted or avoided as practically possible in one's own context.

The Significance of 'Done'

Scrum has an official concept of **Done**, and an unofficial concept of **Ready**. Few renowned proponents of Scrum have suggested the concept to *Ready* to be officially integrated into the official Scrum body of knowledge. This concept applies to the readiness of a Requirement or Product Backlog Item (PBI) to be moved from the Product Backlog into a Scrum Backlog.

In the cycle of development within a Sprint, **Ready** will represent the start of the conversion of a PBI into an actual Product Increment. **Done** represents the end of work, when the product increment is shippable.

The work is **Done** if it meets the acceptance criteria defined in the beginning of the Sprint, and Product Increment so delivered is ready to be shipped or released. The definition of **Done** must comply with the expected business value or purpose of the Sprint.

While *Definition of Done (DoD)* is closely associated with the *Acceptance Criteria (AC)*, these concepts are not the same. The <u>*Acceptance Criteria* relates to the delivered functionality,</u> and whether the *Business Owner* considers the delivered product to be acceptable for release.

On the other hand, **DoD refers to a list of activities or artifacts**, which add verifiable value to the Product; hence, <u>DoD is related to the Product quality</u>. This list typically includes: writing code, design documents, unit testing, integration testing, release notes, etc. The focus is on undertaking any activity, which adds value; while discarding activities, which are wasteful in nature.

> The *Definition of Done (DoD)* is a checklist of activities or artifacts, which must be completed to produce and deliver the product of required value.

In the practical world, there are multiple teams working on the product. They may have different DoDs at different levels:

- DoD for a Feature (or PBI)
- DoD for a Sprint (for multiple PBIs in Sprint)
- DoD for a Release (for potentially shippable product increment)

In case multiple teams work on the same product, they need not have a common Definition of Done.

> All Development Teams must have a definition of "done" that makes their combined work potentially releasable

Several factors influence which of the above categories the activity belongs to. This is determined by asking the following questions:

Can we do this activity for each Feature? If not, can we do it for each Sprint? If not, can we do it for each Release?

If the answer to the first two questions is a 'No', there could be some impediments, which need to be identified and addressed.

The concept of Transparency, Inspection and Adaption applies to the DoD as well. It changes over time, and should be audited and updated from time to time. Additional activities may be added or dropped based on the growing maturity of the team. Also, the DoD is used to validate the tasks in the Sprint Backlog – if all the required or major tasks are accounted for. Finally, as specified earlier, it is used as check list to ensure that all required activities and artifacts are accounted for – at various levels (Feature, Sprint or Release).

Figure 4.1.4: Definition of Done

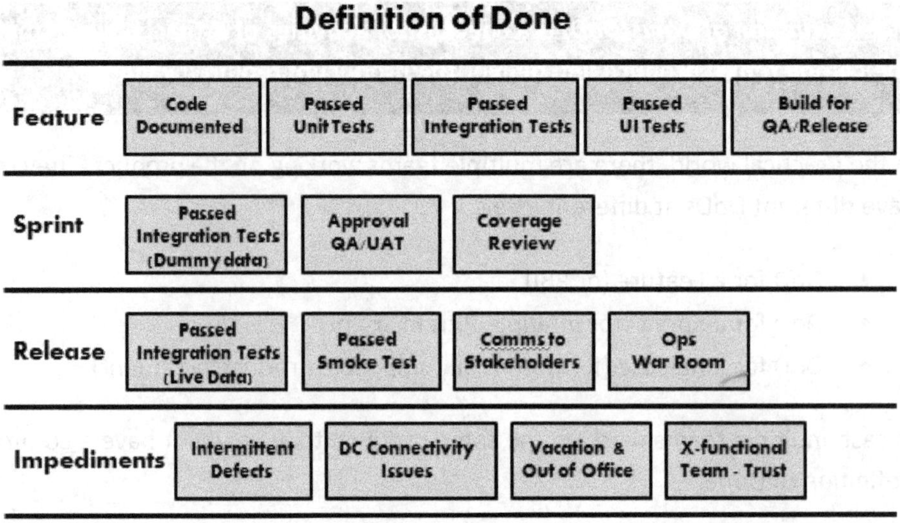

Definition of Done

Feature	Code Documented	Passed Unit Tests	Passed Integration Tests	Passed UI Tests	Build for QA/Release
Sprint	Passed Integration Tests (Dummy data)	Approval QA/UAT	Coverage Review		
Release	Passed Integration Tests (Live Data)	Passed Smoke Test	Comms to Stakeholders	Ops War Room	
Impediments	Intermittent Defects	DC Connectivity Issues	Vacation & Out of Office	X-functional Team - Trust	

There is another controversial concept: Done-Done

Several Scrum teams define **_Done_** at a lower level. For instance, within a Sprint, there are different levels of Done: Requirements Done, Design Done, Development Done, UT done, SIT Done, QA Done, and so forth. This practice has resulted from an incomplete knowledge or misunderstanding of Scrum.

The Five Scrum Values

There are five core Scrum values, which serves as the foundation for the team's processes, interactions and operations:

- Focus
- Courage
- Openness
- Commitment
- Respect

Focus

Rather than attempting to do many things at a point in time, the objective is to focus on the most valuable item or task. Since most activities are collaborative, the team's focus on the right things is very important. The Scrum Master helps the team in this regard by bringing back the team on track if they lose focus.

Courage

Indecision normally arises from ambiguity or lack of authority or accountability. The Scrum framework promotes team to self-organize and make decisions, since the team is empowered. The team develops the courage to tackle any challenge, which comes their way, with a high degree of responsibility and accountability.

Openness

As specified elsewhere, *Transparency* is one of the three pillars of Scrum. This entails a culture of *Openness* within and outside the team. The team works as a whole, and ensures that issues are not brushed under the carpet. On the contrary, these are brought out in the open and dealt with. Truth, trust and transparency will promote this Openness.

Commitment

A self-organizing and collaborative team can only succeed if each member of the team is committed. This results in a high degree of synergistic commitment from the overall team. Without commitment, the team cannot be effectively responsible or accountable. This becomes manifested in team failure at various levels. In case one or more team members are perceived to be less committed, the Scrum Master can mentor them on how to work more effectively and become more committed.

Respect

Each team member must respect other members of the team, or those outside. Prejudices cannot be entertained. There must be no perception than one is more qualified or competent than another; or one can be relied on more than another. It may be possible that a team member is less skilled or experienced than another, but this should not mean that there should be less respected.

Applicability of Scrum

Scrum can be most suitably applied very well in complex environments or solving complex problems. However, a large spectrum of works falls, not in the **Complex** domain, but in the **Complicated** domain as shown in the diagram below.

It is a simplified form of the *Stacey Complexity Graph* or *Stacey Matrix*. Scrum is equally relevant in this domain as well. More information is available in: **More Stacey RD**. *Strategic management and organisational dynamics: the challenge of complexity*. 3rd ed. Harlow: Prentice Hall, 2002.

Figure 4.1.5: Stacey Matrix

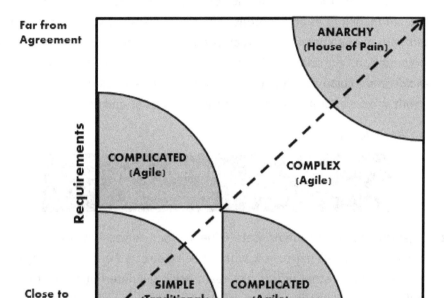

The primary reason why Scrum is considered suitable for *Complicated* and *Complex* projects is because the degree of determinism and predictability becomes lower as we go up the chart diagonally. In contrast, the suitability of empirical models increases.

Typically, such problems are addressed in an *iterative* and *incremental* manner. Rather than resolving all of the problem in one **'big bang'**, it is resolved in **'bits and pieces'**. The parts, for which information is readily available is taken up and addressed first; while seeking more information on the others.

Chapter 2: Scrum Roles

The Scrum Team

In order to focus on the core principles of Scrum, the Scrum Guide describes the Scrum team model, roles and responsibilities and characteristics of the team and its *operations* in quite detail. The structures, purposes and operation of the rest of the organization, outside of the Scrum Team, are not addressed, though *Stakeholders* are cursorily alluded to. A similar approach will be followed in this book, with a few elaboration and clarifications added, as and when required.

Team Characteristics

> **The two principal characteristics of the Scrum Team are:**
> **(a) Self-Organizing, and (b) Cross-functional.**

Self-organizing teams essentially determine, by themselves, how the work will be performed and who will perform it, without being directed or managed by anyone outside the team. In other words, the team itself will determine how the goal is accomplished, within the framework of the formal roles and responsibilities. For instance, collectively and in mutual agreement, the team determines the work-breakdown (typically, from a User Story) into Tasks and assignment of each Task to an individual team member.

The team is considered '**cross-functional**' in the sense that it has all the competencies and skills to accomplish goals and get the work done, without depending on others outside the team. From the formal perspective of the Scrum, this is considered to be true most of the time, under a 'normal' scenario. From a day-to-day perspective, the scrum team does not have to depend on anyone outside the team. However, there may be exceptional situations when an external expert, such a specialized architect or subject-matter-expert may have to be brought into the team for either a temporary period of time, or few ad hoc discussion sessions.

After assessing the above two characteristics, it may be implied that the team is usually 'self-sufficient' in terms of skills and competencies across various roles (business analysts, designer, developer, QA/tester, etc.), technologies or platforms (Java, Unix, C, PHP, Python, etc.) and functions or domains (Sales, Marketing, HR, Finance, etc.). However, do note that most scrum teams are quite often restricted to a single domain or sub-domain (such as 'collections' or 'billing/invoicing' within Finance). It is very common for the same person to play multiple roles of an analyst, UI designer, developer and tester on a particular PBI or some combination of roles across multiple PBIs.

Scrum Teams deliver products **iteratively** and **incrementally**, maximizing opportunities for feedback. Incremental deliveries of "Done" product ensure a potentially useful version of working product is always available.

Team Model

The team performing the work using the Scrum framework is referred to **the Scrum Team**. There may be one or more Scrum teams within an organization, and each team will have only three roles, listed below.

At this point, we will not go into the details of whether one person can fulfill multiple Scrum roles, except to state that only one person is expected to perform only one Scrum role within the same Scrum team. However, the same person may play the same role on different or multiple Scrum teams. This will also be discussed in detail later.

> **There are only 3 formal roles in the Scrum Team: (a) Product Owner, (b) Development Team, and (c) Scrum Master.**

Very often, in the Guide, texts or assessments, there is a reference to just "the team". It is left to the reader's interpretation whether the term refers to the Scrum Team or the Development Team. It is very important to understand the context in which the term is used, to make the right interpretation. I would advise some degree of caution, even while I state that this term is often used to refer to the Scrum Team as a whole, and not just the Development team.

Figure 4.2.1: Scrum Team & Roles

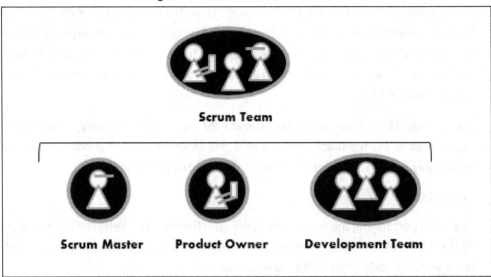

The Scrum Team is envisaged as a **completely flat organization, comprising competent and empowered individuals**. Development Team members do not report to the Scrum Master or the Product Owner. Also, the Scrum Master does not report to the Product Owner, and vice versa. Finally, there's no hierarchy within the Development team.

Scrum Team members are not directed by anyone outside the team. However, **each role has few responsibilities which are clearly defined, which could be interpreted to mean that one role may be directed by another role, internally within the team, and in a particular context**. Few responsibilities may overlap or be shared amongst the different roles. We will discuss these in a subsequent section.

This is because Scrum founders and proponents believe that all *project management* responsibilities are divided between the three roles of Scrum.

Per the Scrum Guide, "each Sprint may be considered a project with no more than a one-month horizon. Like projects, Sprints are used to accomplish something". For *small projects*, like the Sprint described above, the Project Manager responsibilities are *limited*, and may be completely divided amongst the three Scrum roles.

For *large projects*, there are responsibilities, or areas of activities for which the Project Manager is responsible for, which are able and beyond the responsibilities described under Scrum. For purpose of clarity, let us classify a traditional project manager's responsibilities into two categories: (a) scrum responsibilities, and (b) non-scrum responsibilities. Without going into too many details, it should suffice to state that scrum responsibilities have been adequately divided amongst the 3 scrum roles. Non-scrum responsibilities are implicitly assigned to other *stakeholders* (such as a *Development Manager* outside the Scrum Team) from the perspective of Scrum.

Figure 4.2.2: Scrum Teams in an Enterprise

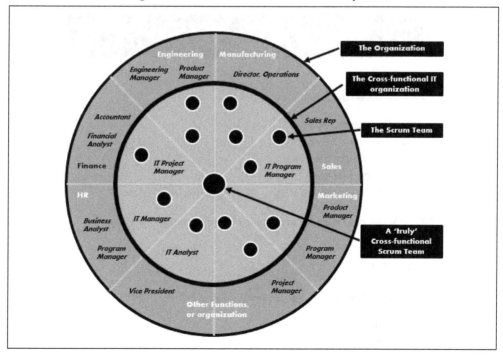

Management of human resources, including reporting relationships, and other resources such as funds are not directly addressed by Scrum. In fact, the issue of hiring and firing the Scrum team is not addressed adequately.

The primary onus of conflict resolution within the Development Team lies within the members of Development team itself. The Scrum Master has the limited authority and responsibility in addressing performance related conflict, unless it arises from a process perspective. In other words, if a team member's poor performance arises from an inadequate understanding of the process, it is the responsibility of the Scrum Master to intervene to improve the process knowledge of the team member. On the other hand, if the conflict arises from a 'discipline' perspective, the team is expected to resolve it internally using fair and mutually-acceptable means. Neither the Scrum Master nor the Product Owner has the responsibility or authority to intervene and resolve a disciplinary issue. As a member of the Scrum Team, either of them can 'help' to address this issue amicably internally. Though Scrum doesn't address this issue directly, it is expected that this issue is addressed by a key stakeholder (e.g. Reporting Manager) when internal team members are not able to address it through informal means.

> **The team model in Scrum is designed to optimize flexibility, creativity, and productivity.**

Q4.2.1: Who is on the Scrum Team?

    A)   The Scrum Master
    B)   The Product Owner
    C)   The Development Team
    D)   Project Manager
    E)   None of the above

Q4.2.2: Scrum does not have a role called "project manager."

    A)   True
    B)   False

Q4.2.3: Scrum Master is a "management" position?

    A)   True
    B)   False

Team Roles and Responsibilities

Product Owner

One of the key roles in the Scrum Team is that of the Product Owner. As the name implies, the **Product Owner owns the product** and is the *key decision maker with respect to most aspects of product development. Typically, this role is played by a Business Stakeholder*, who may be a Product Manager, Program Manager or even a Project Manager. When business stakeholders are severely constrained in terms of time and focus, this role may be carried out by a proxy in the IT organization. In this latter case, the ability of the Product Owner to take decisions, particularly business decisions, is severely restricted; hence, it is strongly advised and required that this role is played by a business decision maker, like the Product Manager or Program Manager.

The Product Owner is an individual and not a team or committee. He or she may represent a team or committee, which in turn may represent all of the business stakeholders and their interests.

> **The Product Owner is the sole and only person responsible and accountable for the Product Backlog.**

The Product Owner is the sole custodian of the Product Backlog. In other words, the Product Owner represents all the interests and needs of all business stakeholders with respect to the product; and is empowered to make any necessary business decision. **No business stakeholder or Executive may directly interact with the Development Team with respect to their work, the Product Backlog or any requirement or need**. These stakeholders and Executives have to work with the Product Owner, on any aspect of the Product backlog e.g. priority, scope, budget, and so on.

The person playing the role of the Product Owner should be senior, experienced and mature enough to not only accept the responsibility and accountability required, but also skilled enough to work with different types of stakeholders at different levels in the organization. Interpersonal skills such as negotiation and conflict resolution skills are critical in the role.

> **The Product Owner is responsible for maximizing the value of the product and the work of the Development Team.**

It is very important to understand that **Scrum is highly focused on minimizing waste and maximizing value of the product as well as work i.e. team efforts.**

One of the main purposes of shorter development cycles is to minimize risk – risk of doing the wrong thing, or in the wrong way, or achieving poor quality. By compressing the timeline, the team effort and cost of an iteration is minimized to some form of 'quanta', even if the whole output is a throw-away. Simultaneously, the focus is on adding or increasing value in each quantum of work so that the value of the output or product is maximized. This value focus is consistent and continuous (as opposed to continual in case of other methodologies). It applies to improvement of the process, the capability of a team member, and the utility of the product.

Product Owner Responsibilities

While the responsibility of managing the Product Backlog is solely the prerogative of the Product Owner, this responsibility may be delegated to the Development Team. In such a case, however, the responsibility may be delegated but not the accountability. The Product Owner will always be accountable for the Product Backlog.

The Product Backlog management responsibilities include:

- Capturing requirements and expressing them into clear Product Backlog Items (PBI)
- Prioritization of the PBIs – ordering PBIs in terms of priority and importance, to most effectively achieve goals and missions and maximizing the ROI
- Value Optimization – optimizing the value of the product and work performed by the Development Team (productivity, efficiency and quality)
- Transparency of the Product Backlog within the Scrum Team as well as outside – it should be visible (using "The Wall"), transparent and clear to all.
- The Product Owner provides the status of the project, and the plans which shows what the Scrum Team will work on next
- The Product Owner clarifies the requirements as expressed in the PBI, and ensures that the Development Team has enough details required to accomplish the work.

The Product Owner manages the Product Backlog, and does not manage the Development Team. It is also very important to note that **only the Product Owner is authorized to abnormally terminate the Sprint**. Typically, the abnormal termination of the Sprint occurs when:

- The current work is no longer necessary, because there is no longer a business need. This could be due to changes in business environment, business goals and focus, policies, etc.
- The quality of the current work/output is far below expectations (e.g. high degree of variance from expected functionality or performance), and starting from scratch makes more sense than rework.

Scrum Master

The Scrum Master is not a Project Manager. He or she is a friend, philosopher, and guide for the Scrum Team. Scrum Masters are also known as *Servant-Leaders*, because they serve the need of the team as well as the organization as a whole. As custodians of the process, they lead Scrum teams from the perspective of ensuring that the team meets its objectives and goals by facilitating the process and removing impediments.

The Scrum Master role is considered a management role, from the perspective of managing the process. The Scrum Master is not a people manager in the traditional sense. He or she is the coach, who continuously mentors the team on the process, including the Scrum Framework, and how it is to be applied effectively. The team is continuously learning and adapting, thereby becoming more productive with time.

While the Scrum Master's responsibilities are many, these can be generally classified into three key responsibilities:

Coach the team to be productive and effective

The Scrum Master first ensures that the team understands the Scrum Framework and applies it correctly. He or she helps the team to identify and adopt a suitable process, or methodologies, which supplement the Scrum Framework. They continually train the team on the Framework and processes, until the team attains a suitable degree of maturity in understanding and implementing them. Scrum Masters train each member of the team on how to perform his or her own responsibility. For instance, they train Product Owners how to manage the Product Backlog; or Developers, how to estimate the effort involved to deliver a Product Backlog Item, or develop a Definition of Done.

The Scrum Master facilitates the work being done, either directly or indirectly, by coaching the team to become more productive and effective. While team itself decides how the work is to be done, the Scrum Master observes and guides the team to perform more efficiently or effectively, if required. This is not achieved by means of directing the team, but prompting the team to discover the right way of doing things. The Scrum Master encourages the adoption of repeatable best practices, which the team may have discovered on its own. He or she helps to identify gaps and prompt the team on how these can be addressed and continually improved. In short, they help the team become better.

Maintain Progress: Keep the team moving forward

The Scrum Master facilitates the attempts of the team to self-organize and collaborate in an effective manner. They protect the team from outside interference and ensures that there are minimal distractions. They are responsible for removing any impediment, which may be blocking the progress of the team. These impediments could be caused or observed internally or externally. For instance, it could be the lack of trust or support of external interdependent teams; or, inability of a team member to adequately perform due to an inadequate knowledge of Scrum or suitable techniques. Scrum Masters may help to facilitate meetings when these are not being conducted properly; not by 'taking over', but by guiding the team to conduct these appropriately.

Help everyone understand Scrum

The Scrum Master is responsible for ensuring that Scrum is understood and implemented correctly. They champion the adoption of Scrum across the organization by spreading knowledge about Scrum, and training people if required. They ensure that the rest of the organization is aware of their own roles and responsibilities required to support Scrum teams. For instance, they may advise external stakeholders how to best support or engage the Scrum teams through Sprint Reviews.

Development Team

Every single member of the Development Team has a single role – Developer. There are no roles or sub-roles called Analyst, Programmer, Tester, and so on. Due to its cross-functional nature, the team possesses all or most of the skills required to perform the work. In exceptional cases, the team may invite specialists to join the team for a short period of time; or, meet as and when required on an ad hoc basis.

The Development Team, collectively and collaboratively, perform the actual work of delivering the Product Increment. A Product Backlog Item cannot be assigned to a Developer. It is owned by the team as a whole, even if discrete tasks may be owned by different team members. The team collectively decides how the work is to be performed and how the work is distributed. There is no concept of 'First Amongst Equals' in the Development Team. In other words, there is no role of a Development Lead.

The optimal size of the Development team is 3-9 members, in addition to the Scrum Master and Product Owner.

While the Product Owner determines the order of priority of Product Backlog Items, and presents a list of Candidate PBIs for the Sprint, the Development team selects the PBIs, which will be delivered in the Sprint. The Development Team also decides HOW the work will be done.

Q4.2.4: What is the recommended size for a Development Team (within the Scrum Team)?

A) Minimal 7
B) 3 to 9
C) 7 plus or minus 2
D) 9

Q4.2.5: What is the primary way a Scrum Master keeps a Development Team working at its highest level of productivity?

A) By facilitating Development Team decisions and removing impediments.
B) By ensuring the meetings start and end at the proper time.
C) By preventing changes to the backlogs once the Sprint begins.
D) By keeping high value features high in the Product Backlog.

Q4.2.6: Who should know the most about the progress toward a business objective or a release, and be able to explain the alternatives most clearly?

    A)   The Product Owner.
    B)   The Development Team.
    C)   The Scrum Master.
    D)   The Project Manager.

Q4.2.7: What is the main reason for the Scrum Master to be at the Daily Scrum?

    A)   To make sure every team member answers the three questions in the right team member order.
    B)   He or she does not have to be there; he or she only has to ensure the Development Team has a Daily Scrum.
    C)   To write down any changes to the Sprint Backlog, including adding new items, and tracking progress on the burndown.
    D)   To gather status and progress information to report to management.

Q4.2.8: The Product Backlog is ordered by:

    A)   Small items at the top to large items at the bottom.
    B)   Safer items at the top to riskier items at the bottom.
    C)   Least valuable items at the top to most valuable at the bottom.
    D)   Items are randomly arranged.
    E)   Whatever is deemed most appropriate by the Product Owner.

Figure 4.2.3: Scrum Roles & Responsibilities

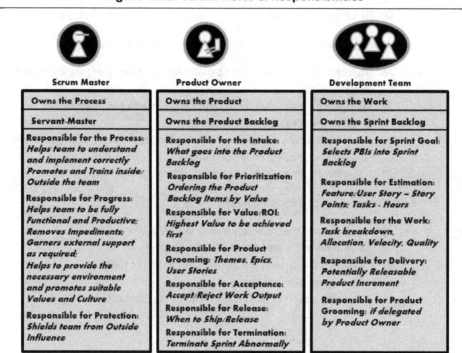

Scrum Master	Product Owner	Development Team
Owns the Process	**Owns the Product**	**Owns the Work**
Servant-Master	**Owns the Product Backlog**	**Owns the Sprint Backlog**
Responsible for the Process: *Helps team to understand and implement correctly Promotes and Trains inside/ Outside the team*	**Responsible for the Intake:** *What goes into the Product Backlog*	**Responsible for Sprint Goal:** *Selects PBIs into Sprint Backlog*
Responsible for Progress: *Helps team to be fully Functional and Productive; Removes Impediments; Garners external support as required; Helps to provide the necessary environment and promotes suitable Values and Culture*	**Responsible for Prioritization:** *Ordering the Product Backlog Items by Value*	**Responsible for Estimation:** *Feature/User Story – Story Points; Tasks - Hours*
	Responsible for Value/ROI: *Highest Value to be achieved first*	**Responsible for the Work:** *Task breakdown, Allocation, Velocity, Quality*
	Responsible for Product Grooming: *Themes, Epics, User Stories*	**Responsible for Delivery:** *Potentially Releasable Product Increment*
Responsible for Protection: *Shields team from Outside Influence*	**Responsible for Acceptance:** *Accept/Reject Work Output*	**Responsible for Product Grooming:** *if delegated by Product Owner*
	Responsible for Release: *When to Ship/Release*	
	Responsible for Termination: *Terminate Sprint Abnormally*	

Chapter 3: Scrum Activities

Per the Scrum Guide, there are **four** _**formal**_ _**events**_ for inspection and adaptation:

- Sprint Planning
- Daily Scrum
- Sprint Review
- Sprint Retrospective

These events are meant to provide an optimal opportunity to enhance transparency for inspection and adaptation. These are the formal prescribed meetings. Each meeting has a distinct or definite objective as well as outcome/s, which we shall discuss shortly.

While the need to optimize the number and duration of meetings is an essential aspect of Scrum, the team could actually have additional meetings to deal with ad hoc issues. For instance, a meeting could be arranged with a domain expert to share detailed functional background of a process. The guiding principle is that the meeting should be useful i.e. it should neither be a distraction for the team nor result in wastage of any kind.

The Scrum Alliance refers to these events as _activities_, and has included a fifth activity in this list: *Product Backlog Refinement*.

Per the Scrum Alliance, the five _formal_ _activities_ are:

- Product Backlog Refinement
- Sprint Planning
- Daily Scrum
- Sprint Review
- Sprint Retrospective

All of these activities are conducted within the boundaries of a Sprint

Q4.3.1: The timebox for a Daily Scrum is?

A) The same time of day every day.
B) Two minutes per person.
C) 4 hours.
D) 15 minutes.
E) 15 minutes for a 4 week sprint. For shorter Sprints it is usually shorter.

Q4.3.2: The maximum length of the Sprint Review (its timebox) is:

A) 2 hours.
B) 4 hours for a monthly Sprint. For shorter Sprints it is usually shorter.
C) As long as needed.
D) 1 day.
E) 4 hours and longer as needed.

Q4.3.3: The timebox for the complete Sprint Planning meeting is?

A) 4 hours.
B) 8 hours for a monthly Sprint. For shorter Sprints it is usually shorter.
C) Whenever it is done.
D) Monthly.

The Sprint

All of these activities, including the Sprint itself, are timeboxed events. In other words, each event has a maximum duration and the event automatically ends when the duration is complete. This is particularly true for the Sprint. Once a Sprint has started, its duration cannot be changed. A new Sprint starts as soon as the previous one ends.

> **The Sprint automatically ends (and the next Sprint starts) at the end of the timebox.**

In case of the other formal events (or, activities), the event can be terminated prior to the expiry of the timebox to avoid wastage. For instance, if the purpose of the Daily Scrum is achieved within 10 minutes, the Daily Scrum can be terminated.

Let's assume that the Sprint duration is initially set as 4 weeks, while the team is in a learning mode. Once the team gains a certain degree of maturity and stability, the duration can be then changed to 2 weeks, or 1 week (the shorter, the better). Once the duration is fixed, it cannot be changed in mid-cycle.

Typically, the duration of each activity is proportional to the duration of the Sprint. The only exception is the *Daily Scrum*, the duration of which is always fixed as 15 minutes. If the duration is anything other than 15 minutes e.g. 30 minutes, the team is NOT implementing Scrum per the formal definition of Scrum.

Table 4.3.1: Duration of Time-boxed Activities

Event/Activity	4-week Sprint	2-week Sprint
• Sprint	4 weeks	2 weeks
• Sprint Planning	8 hours	Shorter (~ 4 hours)
• Daily Scrum	15 minutes	15 minutes
• Sprint Review	4 hours	Shorter (~ 2 hours)
• Sprint Retrospective	3 hours	Shorter (1.5 ~ 2 hours)
• *Product Backlog Refinement*	*4 hours*	*Shorter (~ 2 hours)*

Degree of maturity or stability implies:

- The team is now quite knowledgeable on Scrum, and its various practices
- The team is able to make fairly accurate estimations
- The velocity is more or less stable
- The sizing of the Sprint backlog is optimal i.e. the team is able to deliver all the backlog items within the sprint, per the acceptance criteria
- A well-defined and understood definition of Done

It is extremely important to note that the Sprint is a 'container', which includes all the formal events (or, activities) as well as the Development Work itself. The input to the Sprint is the Sprint Backlog, and the output is the *Potentially Shippable or Potentially Releasable Product Increment*, also known as the **Product Increment**, or just the **Increment**.

Each Sprint results in an *Increment*, but it may not be released at the end of the Sprint; hence, it carries a tag 'potentially releasable'. The decision to release it lies with the PO. Increments are usually bundled and released together at the end of a Release Cycle. The Release Cycle may have 1 Sprint only, or more than one; and, the duration of this cycle is also kept constant. Typically, the scope of the Release is defined early up in the Release Cycle, and constitutes the ***Release Backlog*. The Release Backlog is not yet an official Scrum artifact.**

Q4.3.4: When does the next Sprint begin?

A) Next Monday.
B) Immediately following the next Sprint Planning.
C) When the Product Owner is ready.
D) Immediately after the conclusion of the previous Sprint.

Q4.3.5: It is mandatory that the product increment be released to production at the end of each Sprint.

A) True
B) False

Q4.3.6: The purpose of a Sprint is to produce a done increment of working product.

A) True
B) False

Figure 4.3.1: Sprint Overview

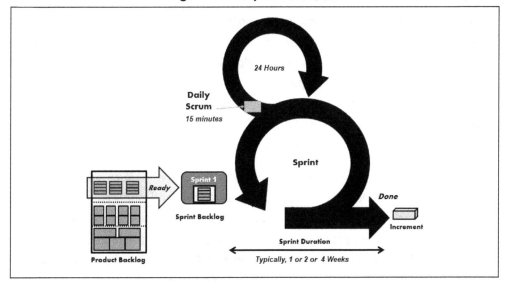

Product Backlog Refinement

The Product Backlog is the single repository for all ideas, needs or requirements for a given Product. It can be considered as an ordered 'Wish List' for the product. Each element in the repository is known as a **Product Backlog Item** (**PBI**), a generalized term that could represent a requirement at different degrees of granularity. While one PBI could be described in highly vague terms in the form of an idea, concept, desire or want, another PBI could be highly specific representing a discrete business rule or policy. See the two examples below:

- The *General Price List* should contain all the *Prices* or *Rates* (including, *Price or Rate Bands*) for all products, software and services being offered through all distribution channels, including direct-to-customers.
- For each *Line item* in an *Invoice*, the *Line Amount* should be calculated per the formula: **Line Amount = Quantity * Price**, where the *Price* is either a discrete *Unit List Price* of the *item*, or an applicable *List Price* in a band, which depends on the *Quantity* purchased.

The Product Backlog contains PBIs at different levels of granularity. Typically, the fine-grained items are towards the top, while larger items are positioned lower. This Ordering is primarily determined by value of the item, its priority and '**readiness'** to be included in a Sprint Backlog.

The Product Backlog Refinement, an iterative process of backlog grooming, makes a PBI **ready** to be included in a Sprint Backlog. When a PBI is ready, it is at a 'right size' – typically, it is a User Story with a size of *n* story points, where *n* is usually 1, 2, 3, 5, … In rare cases, it can be a 'large' User Story, known as an Epic, which can be broken down into smaller User stories after inclusion in the Sprint Backlog. Epics are normally not considered ready.

Usually, the PBI starts large. It is continually analyzed and iteratively decomposed into smaller items; and efforts are estimated. Sometimes, smaller items are merged into one. Very often, value, estimates or priority also changes. These factors determine whether an item moves up or down in the 'list of requirements'. Moreover, new items could get added to, or existing items removed from, the Product Backlog. As a result, this activity is an ongoing, continuous process throughout the Scrum project.

The **Product Backlog exists till the Product exists**. In order for the product to be relevant and competitive, the PBIs change or evolve constantly in response to the market needs. Due to its dynamic and evolving nature, the Product Backlog is never complete or never completely defined. The earliest Sprints starts with the best understood items of that time i.e. what is known, and which is not necessarily complete in terms of all required information to deliver it successfully.

The Product Backlog refinement activity can be considered to precede planning activities, not only because it is a continuous activity, but also because it helps to prepare for upcoming sprints. Very often, this activity is started in advance for at least two sprints, but no more than three or four, when the Sprint is a week-long. There is no formal recommendation for the duration of this meeting, but 2 hours is the norm for a 2-week Sprint, and is usually conducted sometime in the 2nd week.

While the PO is responsible and accountable for the Product Backlog, as well as this activity, the PO may delegate parts of this responsibility to members of the Development Team. Accountability cannot be delegated. The Development team members, essentially, help to define the PBIs better in order to make them Sprint ready. They cannot assign business value or priorities to these items. Neither can they add new items to nor drop existing items from the Product Backlog. In summary, this activity is an ongoing and collaborative exercise; and, never ends, since the Product Backlog is never complete, nor exhausted.

Sprint Planning

Each Sprint starts with the Sprint Planning meeting. It is a timeboxed event of a duration no longer than 8 hours, for a 4-week Sprint. For Sprints with duration less than a month (i.e. less than 4 weeks), the duration of the Sprint Planning meeting is always shorter. The recommended time for this meeting is 2 hours (or less) per week of Sprint duration.

The work to be performed in the Sprint is planned in this meeting. Though most of planning work in this meeting will be performed by the PO and the Development team members, **the entire team** is expected to attend this meeting.

The Scrum Master ensures that:

- The event takes place
- The PO and Development team members attend
- Attendees understand the purpose and outcomes
- Duration is limited to the timebox
- Facilitates the discussion and removes any impediments, if required; for instance, he or she may keep a time-check on each topic on the agenda

Sprint Planning addresses two key points, with respect to the Sprint:

- What to do?
- How to do it?

In other words, this activity provides the results to the following two questions:

- What is the work to be "done" (resulting in an Increment)?
- How will the work be done i.e. a plan?

This activity is guided by the **Sprint Goal**, which is a statement of objective for the Sprint, created during the Sprint Planning meeting.

The Sprint Planning meeting can be considered to have two parts to address each of the two topics listed above, and described below.

Topic 1: What can be done in this Sprint?

In the first part of the meeting, the PO presents the objective the Sprint should achieve and a list of candidate PBIs, the successful delivery of which will lead to achievement of the Sprint Goal, which will be determined shortly. The entire team then collaborates on understanding the "demand" or work required to be done.

The inputs to this process are:

- the Product Backlog (or, a shorter wish list of PBIs, which could be considered for the Sprint),
- the latest product increment, particularly if the development is being done incrementally,
- projected resource capacity of the development team during the Sprint, and
- projected velocity of the development team, based on past performance

While the PO presents the candidate list of PBI items, only the Development team decides the number of items and which items to pick up and include in the Scrum Backlog. This decision is governed by the 'delivery capacity' of the Development team, which only the Development team can assess. The PO cannot dictate or determine which PBIs are selected. In reality, there may be some back-and-forth discussions, or negotiation, between the Development team and PO. The PO influences the selection through the prioritization or ordering of the PBIs, based on the value and priority (urgency).

Another factor that has a significant impact of this selection is whether the PBI is *'ready'*.

The outputs of Part 1 of the meeting are:

- A forecast of the functionality to be delivered in the Sprint, i.e. the PBIs selected to be delivered in the Sprint, and
- The Sprint Goal

Sprint Goal

The Sprint Goal is a statement of objective for the Sprint: what objective will be met by implementation of the selected PBIs and delivering the Increment. In other words, it is a short statement collaboratively written by the Scrum team, which describes what the team wishes to achieve during the Sprint. For example, 'implement basic shopping cart functionality, which allows Users to select of items from a Catalog and add them or remove them from the Cart, or update quantities', the second iteration may 'allow Users to move items from a Shopping Cart into a new or existing Wish List, and vice versa'.

Sprint goals align up with the Product Vision, and Program Objectives. It guides the Development team on why the Increment is being developed. While it allows for some degree of flexibility in the functionality being developed and delivered, it sets the boundaries for achievement of the ultimate goal. This may be in the form of one coherent function or feature; it could be any other coherence that causes the Development team to work together towards the same goal. In a wider context, different Development Teams may work towards the same coherence of a Program Objective.

Topic 2: How will the work get done?

In the next step, the Development Team discusses and decides how the work will be done.

Neither the Scrum Master nor the Product Owner is a required attendee in this part of the meeting. However, it is recommended that the PO participates in this meeting to clarify any doubts or respond to any questions the Development Team may have about the PBIs or functionality to be delivered. The Scrum Master may attend to observe if the process is efficient and effective; and, may intervene, if required to make it so. Neither the PO nor Scrum Master has any authority to determine WHAT work will be done and HOW it will be done by the Development team. The Development team may also invite other stakeholders, whose inputs are needed. This may include technical and domain experts.

As a self-organizing and self-managed unit, the Development team determines the amount of work involved in delivering the Increment. More often than not, team is not required to decompose the PBIs into smaller units e.g. Epics to User Stories; particularly, if the Product Backlog Refinement activity had been undertaken well in the past. The focus is on identifying the work breakdown or task involved in delivering each PBI as part of the Increment; and the effort involved in each task. Typically, User Stories are expressed in terms of Story Points, but Tasks are expressed in hours.

This decomposition of the work for the entire Sprint is the Plan. All the work for the entire Sprint is not planned during the Sprint Planning meeting; so the Sprint Plan is at a 'high-level'. However, the plan for the first few days of the Sprint is adequately detailed. The work to be accomplished in the first few days is broken down in terms of Tasks, which are estimated in hours. Usually, tasks may not exceed a day. Details of the Plan are incrementally added (or corrected) during the course of the Print, when more information or knowledge is gathered or discovered. This planning activity constitutes further analysis of the PBIs and development of an initial design of the system, which may include developing wireframes. These tasks themselves are part of the Plan.

After some degree of planning, the Development Team may determine that there is too much work to be accomplished in the Sprint (or too less). It may renegotiate the scope of work i.e. the PBIs with the PO. By the end of the Planning activity, the Development team should be able to explain to all interested parties how it will work on the PBIs to deliver the Increment. In other words, the Development team should explain the Plan to the PO, Scrum Master, Management, and other interested parties.

The output of the Sprint Planning activity is the Sprint Backlog, which includes the PBIs selected for the Sprint as well as the Plan for the Sprint.

Sprint Backlog = PBIs (for Sprint) + Plan (i.e. Tasks for Sprint)

The Daily Scrum

As the name implies, the Daily Scrum is held on a daily basis. It is timeboxed at 15 minutes, but can be terminated sooner if the objective is achieved. Usually, it is held at the same place and time, so that the team knows where and when it will be held and not require a calendar or schedule. Also, there is a distinct preference amongst practitioners to have this meeting 'the first thing in the morning', typically, 9:00 AM. This is not an explicit requirement, but a norm that seems to have evolved over time. The duration of this meeting cannot exceed 15 minutes, and it is perhaps, the most important *Inspect & Adapt* control point in the Sprint.

> **The Daily Scrum is attended by members of the Development Team, who owns and conducts this meeting.**

The objectives of this meeting are:

- Inspect the work since the last Daily Scrum, and identify improvements if any
- Forecast and plan for the work until the next Daily Scrum, including identification of any impediments (or, risks) and plans to address them

Typically, in this meeting, each Developer in the team explains:

- What did I do yesterday, which helped the Development Team attain the Sprint Goal?
- What will I do today, which will help the Development Team meet the Sprint Goal?
- Do I know of any impediment that prevents me or the Development Team from achieving the Sprint Goal?

As mentioned earlier, the Daily Scrum is perhaps the most important Inspection point during the Sprint. The Development team inspects:

- Progress towards the Sprint Goal, i.e. on track or not
- Progress/trend in completing the work in the Sprint Backlog
- Quality issues, and corrections required
- Impediments, technical or otherwise, which could delay the work or increase risks of not completing the work

On the basis of the discussions, required adaptation is identified and implemented within the Sprint. This ensures that all risks are identified and addressed as early as possible, thereby enhancing the probability of success i.e. meeting the Sprint Goal.

Note that work may be reorganized or Sprint Backlog updated based on the outcome of this meeting. In exceptional cases, PBIs may be refined, added to (or dropped from) the Sprint Backlog in order to complete the work in time, without compromising on the Sprint Goal. Note, however, that Development Team's decision to add/remove PBIs is taken in collaboration with the Product Owner.

Per the Scrum Alliance, the Daily Scrum can be attended by any interested party outside of the Scrum Team; however, only the Scrum Team members are allowed to speak. Scrum Team members include the Scrum Master and the Product Owner.

On the other hand, **per the Scrum Guide, the Daily Scrum is attended by members of the Development Team, who owns and conducts this meeting**. While the Scrum Master may attend, **the PO does not participate in the Daily Scrum**. Other stakeholders are not allowed to participate in the Daily Scrum.

Very often, either few members or the whole Development Team meet immediately after the Daily Scrum for detailed discussions, which cannot and should not be done during the Daily Scrum. The primary objective of this is to discuss in details outcome of the Daily Scrum, and to adapt according during the remainder of the Sprint; or, at least until the next Daily Scrum. **Once the Daily Scrum ends, few members of the Development team can meet with the PO, the Scrum Master, and other stakeholders, if required.**

This helps to address various issues:

- The PO may help to clarify any requirement or issue, if required, *after the Daily Scrum.*
- The Scrum Master can help address any impediment, if required, which may require resources outside the Development Team
- Various stakeholders may provide assistance in the form of knowledge, skills or participation in some dependent activity

The Scrum Master does NOT conduct the Daily Scrum.

The Scrum Master does not have to attend the Daily Scrum meeting. However, it is his responsibility that the meeting does occur every day, and it is being conducted effectively. Nonetheless, it is highly recommended that they attend, because one of the main agendas of this meeting is the *identification and resolution of any impediments* that the Development Team faces. On account of being a 'self-organizing' and 'self-managing' team, the Development Team itself has some degree of responsibility in identifying and removing impediments. Nonetheless, the **final responsibility of resolving impediments rests with the Scrum Master**. The Scrum Master enforces the rule that only Development Team members participate in the Daily Scrum.

There are many advantages of the Daily Scrum:

- All Development team members attend, so it is the best forum to share information and increase knowledge and transparency
- It is a very effective meeting, since everyone is able to share his brief insights even within the limited timeframe
- Everyone is on the same page with respect to the status of work, and remaining plan for achievement of the Sprint Goal
- Impediments, issues and risks are identified and resolved sooner
- Decisions are made in a quick and timely manner
- Collaboration is at its best, resulting in mutual trust and higher performance
- It reduces the need for many meetings to just a few

The Sprint Review

The Sprint Review is conducted at the end of the Sprint, and is the *penultimate* event in the Sprint (the *ultimate* or *last* event is the Sprint Retrospective). It is a timeboxed event attended by the Scrum Team, and all interested stakeholders. **For a 4-week Sprint, the duration is 4 hours**; for Sprints with shorter duration, it is usually shorter. Per the Scrum Alliance, the duration is 1 hour per 1 week of Sprint. The Scrum Master ensures that:

- the event takes place, and is conducted effectively
- each attendee understands its purpose
- duration is limited to the timebox

The primary purpose of this event is to **collaboratively review the Product Increment produced during the Sprint**. The other purpose of the event is to **collaboratively update the Product Backlog**, based on:

- Outcomes and learning from the Sprint, e.g. deferred functionality, improvements identified, etc.
- New or relevant information from outside the Scrum Team, e.g. evolving market needs, defunct features, etc.

Anyone who has a stake in the Product, or its Increment, should get a chance to speak and participate in this meeting. The Scrum Team members and stakeholders collaborate on what was done in the Sprint, as well as what needs to be done going forward. They focus on optimizing value by developing the Product Backlog further.

This is not a Status Meeting, but an informal meeting where the purpose is to review the Increment to elicit feedback and foster collaboration. Typically, the meeting addresses the following elements:

- It usually starts with the Product Owner making a brief statement about the Sprint, the Sprint Goal and the Product Increment
  - What PBIs were Done
  - What was not done

- The Development Team presents a Demo of the Increment, and answers questions on the Increment
- The Development Team discusses what went well during the Sprint, and what did not – what problems were encountered and how they were solved
- The Product Owner discusses the Product Backlog, in its current state, and how much time will be required to complete it based on current rate of progress
- An open discussion between all the participants on what should be done next, and how to update the Product Backlog, based on:
  - Feedback on market: need, potential use, purpose, value
  - Review of timeline, budget, resources, potential capabilities, market for next release
- The Product Owner incorporates appropriate feedback into the Product Backlog:
  - Updates for the short-term (PBIs for next few Sprints)
  - Updates for long-term (new features, promote/demote/drop, etc.)

The Sprint Retrospective

While the Sprint Review was completely focused on the Product, the Sprint Retrospective is focused on the Process. The Sprint Retrospective provides an ideal opportunity to *inspect* itself and *adapt* by developing and implementing a plan to improve itself.

It is a timeboxed event attended by the Scrum Team. It follows the Sprint Review and precedes the Sprint Planning event.

For a 4-week Sprint, the duration is 3 hours; for Sprints with shorter duration, it is usually shorter. Per the Scrum Alliance, the duration is 1 hour per 1 week of Sprint. The Scrum Master participates as a peer team member in the meeting from the accountability over the Scrum process. The Scrum Master also ensures that:

- the event takes place, and is conducted effectively
- each attendee understands its purpose
- duration is limited to the timebox

The primary objectives of the Sprint Retrospective are:

- Inspect what went well (and what didn't go so well) during the last Sprint, with respect to people, relationships, process and tools
- Identify and order the items that went well, so that these can be 'imbibed and embedded into the genes' of the team
- Identify items that didn't go so well to determine potential improvements, and how to effectively adapt them
- Create a Plan for implementing improvements to way the work is done

Note that the Scrum team, on account of its self-organizing and self-managing nature, improves its own process versus relying on others to provide direction. The Scrum Master is a key player in this activity. He or she is responsible for the Scrum Team to continually inspect, learn, adapt and improve; particularly, in terms of the process framework, and the development process and practices. In time, the team become more efficient and effective; and starts to enjoy the work or the process. During each Sprint retrospective, the Scrum Team plans ways and means to improve product quality; for instance, adapting the definition of "Done" as increasingly stringent over Sprints, or increasing the velocity without compromising quality. It is expected that by the end of the Sprint Retrospective, the Scrum Team has identified improvements that it will implement in the next Sprint. Thus, the Sprint Retrospective is a very important event where the concept of *Inspect and Adapt* is directly and formally applied.

Q4.3.7: Why is the Daily Scrum held at the same time and same place?

  A) The place can be named.
  B) The consistency reduces complexity and overhead.
  C) The Product Owner demands it.
  D) Rooms are hard to book and this lets it be booked in advance.

Q4.3.8: Which statement best describes the Sprint Review?

  A) It is a review of the team's activities during the Sprint.
  B) It is when the Scrum Team and stakeholders inspect the outcome of the Sprint and figure out what to do in the upcoming Sprint.
  C) It is a demo at the end of the Sprint for everyone in the organization to provide feedback on the work done.
  D) It is used to congratulate the Development Team if it did what it committed to doing, or to punish the Development Team if it failed to meet its commitments.

Q4.3.9: An abnormal termination of a Sprint is called when?

  A) When it is clear at the end of a Sprint that everything won't be finished.
  B) When the Team feels that the work is too hard.
  C) When Sales has an important opportunity.
  D) When the Product Owner determines that it makes no sense to finish it.

Figure 4.3.2: Formal Sprint Events

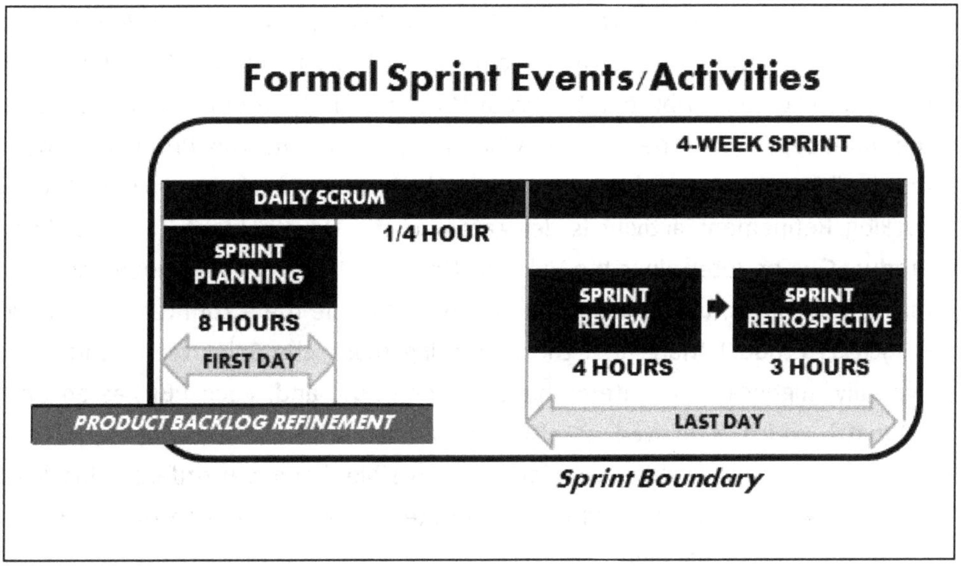

Formal Sprint Events/Activities

Chapter 4: Scrum Artifacts

Product Backlog

The Product Backlog is a single repository in which all the requirements of the product are stored. Each of these requirements is known as a Product Backlog Item (PBI). It is owned and managed by the Product Owner. It can be considered a list of requirements, ordered in terms of value and priority by the Product Owner. Any stakeholder can contribute to the Product Backlog, but it is only Product Owner as the gatekeeper, who determines what goes in or out. The Product Owner is responsible and accountable for managing the Product Backlog, even if the Product Backlog Refinement activity is delegated to the Development Team. Only the Product Owner determines the Value or Order of the PBIs, even though he or she may get critical inputs from other stakeholders inside the Scrum team, or outside – such as Product Managers, the Marketing team, the Sales team, and so on. Typically, higher-ordered items have higher value; and, each PBI has an effort estimate, which is arrived at after discussions with the Development Team. However, if the list of PBIs is very long, it is possible that lower-ordered PBIs do not have an estimate. These estimates are determined at the time of the Product Backlog Refinement activity.

The Development Team's activity is determined by the Product Backlog. Development Team cannot work on any requirement or task, which is not in the Sprint Backlog, which in turn depends entirely on the Product Backlog. Each requirement may be in the form of a desired feature, enhancement, defect or bug fix, and documentation requirements. Each PBI in the Product Backlog may be at different levels of granularity or details. Typically, higher-ordered PBIs at the top of the pile are more detailed than those at the bottom, which are quite vague or are at a 'high-level'. The Product Backlog Refinement activity helps to add more details to the higher-ordered PBIs in an incremental fashion. This may require large items to be broken down into smaller items, or vice versa.

The Product Backlog may, initially, begin as a short list or a very long one. However, it continues to exist until the lifetime of the product, and list is never 'exhausted'. The only exception is in the case of End-of-life of a product, i.e. when the product is discontinued, the Product Backlog will also cease to exist.

> **All business requirements and needs are reflected in the Product Backlog, which is a single repository of all requirements for the product.**

There should, ideally, be **one Product Backlog for one product**. Even if there are different scrum teams working on the same product, there should be only one Product Backlog, which all these teams will work out of. However, *when variants of the same product are treated as different products on account of market segments, features, price, etc., this decision becomes complicated*. The single Product Backlog rule should apply if these products share most of the core functionality and features, without adding too much complexity while resolving 'version' requirements; or, if the scope and number of requirements does not become overwhelming and confusing to manage within one Product Backlog.

In practice, requirements for several 'small' interrelated products, which are developed by a fairly large common team, may also use a common Product Backlog.

For more details, see section on *Product Backlog Refinement* in Chapter 3.

Q4.4.1: When multiple teams are working together, each team should maintain a separate Product Backlog.

A) True
B) False

Q4.4.2: How much work must a Development Team do to a Product Backlog item it selects for a Sprint?

A) As much as it has told the Product Owner will be done for every Product Backlog item it selects in conformance with the definition of done.
B) As much as it can fit into the Sprint.
C) The best it can do given that it is usually impossible for QA to finish all of the testing that is needed to prove shippability.
D) Analysis, design, programming, testing and documentation.

Q4.4.3: Development Team members volunteer to own a Sprint Backlog item:

A)   At the Sprint planning meeting.
B)   Never. All Sprint Backlog Items are "owned" by the entire Development Team, even though each one may be done by an individual development team member.
C)   Whenever a team member can accommodate more work.
D)   During the Daily Scrum.

The Sprint Goal is to transform a Product Backlog Item into a Product Increment.

Figure 4.4.1: Product Backlog to Product Increment

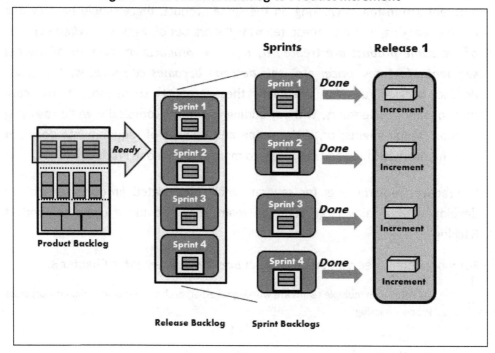

Sprint Backlog

When PBIs are 'ready', they are considered for inclusion in the Sprint Backlog. This is primarily driven by the Order or Priority assigned by the Product Owner. There is a very common misunderstanding that the Product Owner decides what gets into the Sprint Backlog. This is not completely true, and is explained below.

The Product Owner presents the candidate PBIs to the Development team, based on the Order or priority of the PBI. In most cases, the effort estimate of each PBI is already made. Note that this is not a rigorous estimate; and as the name states, just an estimate based on knowledge about the PBI at that time. Another effort estimate may be quickly made at this time, particularly, if the PBI has been in the Product Backlog for a fairly long time; or if the previous estimate was done quite a long time back.

Also, note that, when a PBI from a previous Sprint gets back into the Product Backlog (sine it was not 'done' in the Sprint), a re-estimate may be needed. Of course, only if the PBI continues to be relevant and considered important enough to be a higher-ordered PBI.

The total effort is then compared with the team capacity i.e. velocity, in order to select the final list of the PBIs. The Development Team actually decides which PBIs to pick. In case of any disagreement on the PBIs being selected, there is a negotiation between the Product Owner and the Development Team.

The Development Team cannot pick any PBI from the Product Backlog, but only from amongst the list that the Product Owner presented as a candidate list for the Sprint Goal.

Once the PBIs are selected, a plan is formulated to determine the work required to be done to create the Product Increment. This is part of the Sprint Backlog.

Sprint Backlog = PBIs (for Sprint) + Plan (i.e. Tasks for Sprint)

The Sprint Backlog is an output of the Sprint Planning activity, and includes the PBIs selected for the Sprint as well as the Plan for the Sprint.

The Product Increment

Each successful Sprint results in the delivery of the Product Increment. It comprises the sum-total of all PBIs as implemented in the current sprint.

Very often, it is considered that Product Increment is an aggregated total i.e. increment delivered in the current Sprint + all increments developed in all previous sprints. This is not necessarily true. Multiple teams may work on multiple branches of the code and they are merged only per the Release Plans. This is not in the scope of our discussions.

The name Product Increment comes from the fact that Product is indeed being developed incrementally and iteratively.

For it to be considered complete, it must meet the following criteria:

- It must be "done", as defined in the team's current definition of done
- It must meet the Product Owner's Acceptance Criteria, as defined early in the Sprint
- It must meet the value envisaged or defined at the beginning of the Sprint.

For it to be potentially releasable, it must meet the following criteria:

- It must still be relevant to market needs, with no degradation in priority

Whether it actually gets released depends on other factors beyond the control of the Scrum Team. It depends on collective decision making between the Product Owner, Product Managers and the Release team/s.

Finally, it is important to note that it's not only the software, which is being delivered as part of the Product Increment. All required artifacts, as specified in the Definition of Done, have to be delivered as well.

Part 5: Practice Q&A

Q5.1: Which statement best describes Scrum?

    A) A complete methodology that defines how to develop software.

    B) A cookbook that defines best practices for software development.

    C) A framework within which complex products in complex environments are developed.

    D) A defined and predictive process that conforms to the principles of Scientific Management.

Q5.2: When many Development Teams are working on a single product, what best describes the definition of "done?"

    A) Each Development Team defines and uses its own. The differences are discussed and reconciled during a hardening Sprint.

    B) Each Development Team uses its own but must make their definition clear to all other Teams so the differences are known.

    C) All Development Teams must have a definition of "done" that makes their combined work potentially releasable.

    D) It depends.

Q5.3: What is the maximum length of a Sprint?

    A) Not so long that the risk is unacceptable to the Product Owner.

    B) Not so long that other business events can't be readily synchronized with the development work.

    C) No more than one calendar month.

    D) All of these answers are correct.

Q5.4: What is the role of Management in Scrum?

    A) To continually monitor staffing levels of the Development Team.

    B) To monitor the Development Team's productivity.

    C) Management supports the Product Owner with insights and information into high value product and system capabilities. Management supports the Scrum Master to cause organizational change that fosters empiricism, self-organization, bottom-up intelligence, and intelligent release of software.

D) To identify and remove people that aren't working hard enough.

Q5.5: Development Team membership should change:

A) Every Sprint to promote shared learning.
B) Never, because it reduces productivity.
C) As needed, while taking into account a short term reduction in productivity.
D) Just as it would on any development team, with no special allowance for changes in productivity.

Q5.6: During a Sprint, a Development Team determines that it will not be able to finish the complete forecast. Who should be present to review and adjust the Sprint work selected?

A) The Scrum Master, the project manager and the Development Team.
B) The Product Owner and the Development Team.
C) The Product Owner and all stakeholders.
D) The Development Team.

Q5.7: Which two (2) things does the Development Team not do during the first Sprint?

A) Deliver an increment of potentially shippable functionality.
B) Nail down the complete architecture and infrastructure.
C) Develop and deliver at least one piece of functionality.
D) Develop a plan for the rest of the project.

Q5.8: The Development Team should have all the skills needed to:

A) Complete the project as estimated when the date and cost are committed to the Product Owner.
B) Do all of the development work, but not the types of testing that require specialized testing, tools, and environments
C) Turn the Product Backlog items it selects into an increment of potentially shippable product functionality.

Q5.9: The Development Team should not be interrupted during the Sprint. The Sprint Goal should remain intact. These are conditions that foster creativity, quality and productivity. Based on this, which of the following is false?

A) The Product Owner can help clarify or optimize the Sprint when asked by the Development Team.
B) The Sprint Backlog and its contents are fully formulated in the Sprint Planning meeting and do not change during the Sprint.
C) As a decomposition of the selected Product Backlog Items, the Sprint Backlog changes and may grow as the work emerges.
D) The Development Team may work with the Product Owner to remove or add work if it finds it has more or less capacity than it expected.

Q5.10: Who is responsible for registering the work estimates during a Sprint?

A) The Development Team.
B) The Scrum Master.
C) The Product Owner.
D) The most junior member of the Team.

Q5.11: An organization has decided to adopt Scrum, but management wants to change the terminology to fit with terminology already used. What will likely happen if this is done?

A) Without a new vocabulary as a reminder of the change, very little change may actually happen.
B) The organization may not understand what has changed with Scrum and the benefits of Scrum may be lost.
C) Management may feel less anxious.
D) All answers apply.

Q5.12: Who is required to attend the Daily Scrum?

A) The Development Team.
B) The Scrum team.
C) The Development Team and Scrum Master.
D) The Development Team and Product Owner.

E) The Scrum Master and Product Owner.

Q5.13: During the Daily Scrum, the Scrum Master's role is to:

A) Lead the discussions of the Development Team.
B) Make sure that all 3 questions have been answered.
C) Manage the meeting in a way that each team member has a chance to speak.
D) Teach the Development Team to keep the Daily Scrum within the 15 minute timebox.
E) All of the above.

Q5.14: What is the main reason for the Scrum Master to be at the Daily Scrum?

A) To make sure every team member answers the three questions in the right team member order.
B) He or she does not have to be there; he or she only has to ensure the Development Team has a Daily Scrum.
A) To write down any changes to the Sprint Backlog, including adding new items, and tracking progress on the burndown.
B) To gather status and progress information to report to management.

Q5.15: The CEO asks the Development Team to add a "very important" item to the current Sprint. What should the Development Team do?

A) Add the item to the current Sprint without any adjustments.
B) Add the item to the current Sprint and drop an item of equal size.
C) Add the item to the next Sprint.
D) Inform the Product Owner so he/she can work with the CEO.

Correct Answers

Question #	Correct Answers
1	C
2	C
3	D
4	C
5	C
6	B
7	B, D
8	C
9	B
10	A
11	D
12	A
13	D
14	B
15	D

Part 6: Fast-Track Review Sheets

6.1 Important Points to Remember

- Scrum framework is based on the EMPIRICAL process control theory.

- The EMPIRICAL process theory relies on current knowledge and experience to analyze the work being done (work-breakdown) or determine the plan on how the work will be done

- The three pillars of Scrum are: Transparency, Inspection and Adaptation

- The five core Scrum Values are: Focus, Courage, Openness, Commitment and Respect.

- Scrum is suitable for Complex and Complicated systems and environments.

- There are only 3 Roles in Scrum: Product Owner, Scrum Master, Development Team

- There is no role of Project Manager in Scrum.

- The Scrum Master role is considered a Management role, because s/he manages the Process.

- The Scrum Master is responsible for the Process, the Product Owner for the Product (and the Product Backlog) and the Development for the Work (or Product Increment)

- There can be only 3-9 members in the Development Team.

- Only the Product Owner decides what is in the Product Backlog

- The Product Owner decides the priority or Order of the PBIs.

- The Product Owner is responsible for Product Backlog Refinement. This can be delegated to the Development Team, but the Product Owner continues to be accountable for the Product Backlog (management).

- A timeboxed event refers to the fact that the event can take no more than a maximum amount of time

- Typically, the duration of a Sprint is one of the following: One Week or Two Weeks or Four Weeks (i.e. One Month)

- A shorter Sprint Duration is generally considered as better.

- The next sprint starts as soon as the previous one ends

- Per the Scrum Alliance, the five formal activities for inspection and adaptation are: (a) Product Backlog Refinement, (b) Sprint Planning, (c) Daily Scrum, (d) Sprint Review, and (e) Sprint Retrospective

- All of these activities are conducted within the boundaries of a Sprint

- The Definition of Done (DoD) is a checklist of activities or artifacts, which must be completed to produce and deliver the product of required value.

- All Development Teams must have a definition of "done" that makes their combined work potentially releasable

- The two principal characteristics of the Scrum Team are: (a) Self-Organizing, and (b) Cross-functional.

- The team model in Scrum is designed to optimize flexibility, creativity, and productivity.

- The Product Owner is an individual and not a team or committee

- The same person cannot be the Scrum Master as well as the Product Owner.

- Value Maximizer: The Product Owner is responsible for maximizing the value of the product and the work of the Development Team.

- Only the Product Owner is authorized to abnormally terminate the Sprint. S/he may be advised by Scrum Master or Development Team to do so.

- The primary way a Scrum Master keeps a Development Team working at its highest level of productivity is by facilitating Development Team decisions and removing impediments.

- The Sprint Goal is a statement of objective for the Sprint: what objective will be met by implementation of the selected PBIs and delivering the Increment

- This decomposition of the work for the entire Sprint is the Plan

- Sprint Backlog = PBIs (for Sprint) + Plan (i.e. Tasks for Sprint)

- The Daily Scrum is attended by members of the Development Team, who owns and conducts this meeting

- The Scrum Master or PO does not have to participate in the Daily Scrum.

- Per the Scrum Alliance, the Daily Scrum can be attended by any interested party outside of the Scrum Team; however, only the Scrum Team members are allowed to speak.

- The Scrum Master does NOT conduct the Daily Scrum.

- The Scrum Master does not have to attend the Daily Scrum meeting, but only ensure that it gets done.

- Very often, either few members or the whole Development Team meet immediately after the Daily Scrum for detailed discussions

- There are three artifacts: (a) Product Backlog, (b) Sprint Backlog, and (c) Product Increment

- All business requirements and needs are reflected in the Product Backlog, which is a single repository of all requirements for the product

- There is only one Product Backlog for one Product.

- Product Owner selects PBIs for potential inclusion into Sprint Backlog.

- The Development teams selects from the above list what it can accommodate in the Sprint. This becomes the Sprint Backlog.

- Development Team cannot pick any item from the Product Backlog directly, unless the Backlog Management responsibility is delegated to them.

- No one can work on anything not included in the Sprint Backlog.

- In other words, no one can work on anything not included in the Product Backlog.

- Management cannot include anything in the Product Backlog without the agreement of the Product Owner.

6.2 Important Diagrams to Remember

Manifesto for Agile Software Development

We are uncovering better ways of developing
software by doing it and helping others do it.
Through this work we have come to value:

Individuals and interactions over *processes and tools*

Working software over *comprehensive documentation*

Customer collaboration over *contract negotiation*

Responding to change over *following a plan*

That is, while there is value in the items on
the right, we value the items on the left more.

Principles behind the Agile Manifesto

We follow these principles:

Our highest priority is to satisfy the customer
through early and continuous delivery
of valuable software.

Welcome changing requirements, even late in
development. Agile processes harness change for
the customer's competitive advantage.

Deliver working software frequently, from a
couple of weeks to a couple of months, with a
preference to the shorter timescale.

Business people and developers must work
together daily throughout the project.

Build projects around motivated individuals.
Give them the environment and support they need,
and trust them to get the job done.

The most efficient and effective method of
conveying information to and within a development
team is face-to-face conversation.

Working software is the primary measure of progress.

Agile processes promote sustainable development.
The sponsors, developers, and users should be able
to maintain a constant pace indefinitely.

Continuous attention to technical excellence
and good design enhances agility.

Simplicity--the art of maximizing the amount
of work not done--is essential.

The best architectures, requirements, and designs
emerge from self-organizing teams.

At regular intervals, the team reflects on how
to become more effective, then tunes and adjusts
its behavior accordingly

In the example below, the Release is planned in advance – before Sprint 1 – and the Release Backlog is identified, with the four Sprint Backlogs.

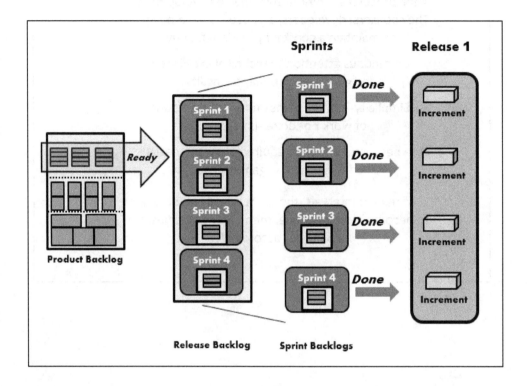

At the end of each Sprint, the Sprint Backlog (and hence, the Release Backlog) may be re-visited and revised.

There will be only one Release, after the fourth Sprint, when all four Increments are made available.

The Sprint: From Ready (PBI) to Done (Increment)

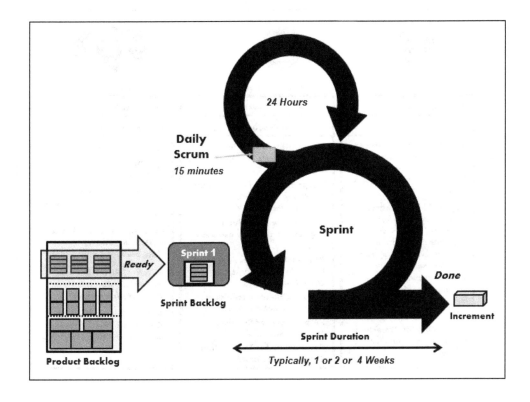

Roles & Key Responsibilities

Scrum Master

Product Owner

Development Team

Owns the Process	Owns the Product	Owns the Work
Servant-Master	**Owns the Product Backlog**	**Owns the Sprint Backlog**
Responsible for the Process: *Helps team to understand and implement correctly Promotes and Trains inside/Outside the team*	**Responsible for the Intake:** *What goes into the Product Backlog*	**Responsible for Sprint Goal:** *Selects PBIs into Sprint Backlog*
Responsible for Progress: *Helps team to be fully Functional and Productive; Removes Impediments; Garners external support as required; Helps to provide the necessary environment and promotes suitable Values and Culture*	**Responsible for Prioritization:** *Ordering the Product Backlog Items by Value*	**Responsible for Estimation:** *Feature/User Story – Story Points; Tasks - Hours*
	Responsible for Value/ROI: *Highest Value to be achieved first*	**Responsible for the Work:** *Task breakdown, Allocation, Velocity, Quality*
	Responsible for Product Grooming: *Themes, Epics, User Stories*	**Responsible for Delivery:** *Potentially Releasable Product Increment*
	Responsible for Acceptance: *Accept/Reject Work Output*	**Responsible for Product Grooming:** *if delegated by Product Owner*
Responsible for Protection: *Shields team from Outside Influence*	**Responsible for Release:** *When to Ship/Release*	
	Responsible for Termination: *Terminate Sprint Abnormally*	

Duration of Key Events for 4-week Sprint

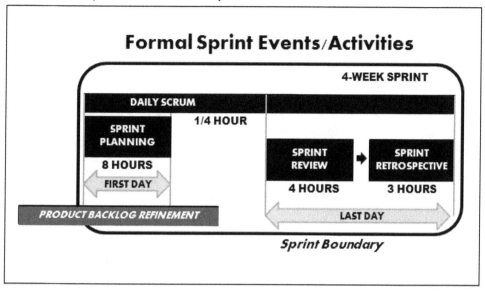

CPSIA information can be obtained
at www.ICGtesting.com
Printed in the USA
BVHW010453101219
566107BV00021B/90/P